CALM

AMIDST

CHAOS

*A Frontline Memoir of the Palisades Fire
and the Voice That Guided a City*

ERIK SCOTT

Los Angeles Fire Captain & Public Information Officer

the three
tomatoes
Book Publishing

Published December 2025

Paperback ISBN: 979-8-9931598-6-7
Hardcover ISBN: 979-8-9931598-7-4
eBook ISBN: ISBN: 979-8-9931598-9-8

Library of Congress Control Number: 2025924758

For information address:
The Three Tomatoes Book Publishing
6 Soundview Rd.
Glen Cove, NY 11542

Cover design: Susan Herbst
Interior design: Susan Herbst
Cover photo: Richard Diede
Author Photo: Lauren Scott
Photographs courtesy of the contributors. All rights reserved.
Used with permission.

Oscar® and Academy Awards® are registered trademarks of the Academy of Motion Picture Arts and Sciences. SAG Awards® is a registered trademark of SAG-AFTRA. Golden Globe® is a registered trademark of the Hollywood Foreign Press Association. All other trademarks are the property of their respective owners. No endorsement is implied.

Disclaimer:
This memoir reflects Erik Scott's personal experiences during the 2025 Palisades Fire. The views expressed are solely his own and do not represent the Los Angeles Fire Department, the City of Los Angeles, or any other organization. Dialogue and events may be reconstructed; while accuracy has been sought, this account reflects one individual's perspective and should not be considered professional firefighting, medical, or legal advice. All referenced information is publicly available, and no confidential sources were used. Some passages describe traumatic events and may be difficult to read.

This book was written independently, self-funded, and created on personal time, without financial support from any public agency or organization.

Any appearance of official uniforms, equipment, insignia, or trademarks is incidental to documenting real events. No agency or department has endorsed or participated in this book, and individuals are included only as part of factual events without implying endorsement.

"Every firefighter wearing a badge—every officer—was doing everything they possibly could. We met circumstances beyond our control. There were countless individual acts of bravery and dedication that will never make a headline, but they were there— every day."

~ *Margaret Stewart, Firefighter & Public Service Officer*

PRAISE FOR CALM AMIDST CHAOS

"As Mayor of Los Angeles, I stood side by side with Captain Erik Scott as we worked through some of our city's most challenging emergencies—from wildfires to windstorms. He has a gift for humanizing crises, his steady communication kept Angelenos informed and reassured when they needed it most. *Calm Amidst Chaos* is a powerful reflection and moving story of that same grace under pressure."

~ Eric Garcetti, Former Mayor of Los Angeles,
and U.S. Ambassador to India

"When breaking news unfolds in Los Angeles, Captain Erik Scott is the voice journalists trust. His consistency, accuracy, and humanity have set the standard for public communication. *Calm Amidst Chaos* takes you behind the cameras to show how leadership and empathy can save lives."

~ Robert Kovacik, Anchor & Reporter, NBC Los Angeles

"I've served alongside Erik Scott for more than two decades. He's a firefighter's firefighter—a credible officer who leads with both head and heart. *Calm Amidst Chaos* honors every first responder who has ever stood between danger and the people they protect."

~ Frank Lima, General Secretary-Treasurer,
International Association of Fire Fighters

"I drove through the fire with my four-month-old son in the backseat and later worked nonstop to help our community find reliable information. During that chaos, Captain Erik Scott's updates were our constant. His clarity and willingness to share what we needed—often before we asked—helped steady an entire community."

~ Larry Vein, Founder, Pali Strong

Dedication

This book is dedicated to the twelve individuals who lost their lives in the Palisades Fire. It is also dedicated to the countless residents whose lives were forever changed, to the outstanding work of the firefighters and first responders who faced unprecedented conditions, and to all the untold stories of bravery and resilience that may never fully be known.

Foreword

I've been through fires before. I've stood in the ashes of my own burned-down home, and I've seen disaster up close in places like Haiti, New Orleans, and during the COVID crisis when our team at CORE worked around the clock at Dodger Stadium. You learn a lot about humanity in those moments—who steps forward, who stays steady, and who people look to when everything feels uncertain.

The Palisades Fire was one of those moments when a community was tested so intensely that its character was revealed in the clearest possible terms. I watched families lose homes, neighbors rise to help one another, and first responders fight an unprecedented force of nature with skill, courage, and resolve. And in the middle of it all was Captain Erik Scott—a calm, trusted voice guiding a shaken community through smoke, fear, and confusion.

I've known Erik through our work with CORE, where I saw the same qualities that fill these pages: clarity, compassion, and an unshakable sense of responsibility to the people he serves. Later, when we walked the burnt streets of the Palisades together, I watched him pause interviews to help residents who needed answers or comfort. His focus is clear. That's who he is—whether the cameras are on him or no one is watching.

Erik Scott

Calm Amidst Chaos is not just the story of a fire. It's a chronicle of leadership under pressure, of firefighters who refused to surrender to impossible conditions, and of a community that held together when everything else was falling apart. Erik takes you into the air with the pilots, onto the line with the crews, and into the quieter moments that rarely make the news but say the most about who we are when it counts.

The firefighters and public safety professionals of Los Angeles are among the best in the world. Their work is often unseen, their sacrifices often unspoken. This book gives them the light they deserve. It honors not only the men and women on the frontline, but also the families, neighbors, and community members who carried the weight long after the flames were out.

Erik tells their stories with accuracy and heart because he lived them—day after day, night after night. And in doing so, he reminds us that the noblest form of service is steady and entirely human.

It's a privilege to stand behind this work, and an honor to lend my voice to it.

~ *Sean Penn, actor, filmmaker, humanitarian*

TABLE OF CONTENTS

Preface.. 1

Prologue... 3

Part 1: The Frontline in Action

Chapter 1: The Calm Before the Fire 9

Chapter 2: Into the Inferno 15

Chapter 3: The Horn in the Dark....................................... 23

Chapter 4: The Sky Above the Fire.................................... 33

Chapter 5: The Iron Line 43

Chapter 6: The Lifeline of Logistics.................................. 51

Chapter 7: The Weight of the Flames 57

Chapter 8: The Calm Voice 61

Chapter 9: Off-Duty Courage... 79

Photos Part 1 87

Part 2: Recovery, Mudslides, Resilience

Chapter 10: The Long Tail of Recovery............................. 99

Chapter 11: Resilience.. 109

Chapter 12: The Neighborhood Chief................................ 121

Chapter 13: After the Fire, Recovery, and the Rains 129

Chapter 14: The Weight We Carry 139

Photos: Part 2 145

Part 3: From Ashes to the Spotlight

Chapter 15: Invitations to Hollywood's Biggest Stages 155

Chapter 16: The Oscars.. 161

Chapter 17: The Los Angeles Press Club 167

Photos for Part 3 177

Part 4: Closure, Lessons, Leadership, Reflection

Chapter 18: Cause and Closure 189
Chapter 19: The After-Action Review 199
Chapter 20: Chiefs' Playbook for a Wind-Driven City 209
Chapter 21: Unified LA: One Clear Voice 213
Chapter 22: Lessons in Disaster Preparedness 217
Chapter 23: Leadership Under Fire 225
Chapter 24: Reflection and Resolve 233
Photos for Part 4 237

Epilogue 243
Acknowledgements 245
About the Author 247

Preface

In the heart of every crisis lies a story of resilience—one that demands to be told, not just remembered. Catastrophe has a way of stripping away the noise, revealing the raw essence of human character. The Pacific Palisades Fire of January 2025 was one such moment—a flashpoint when the City of Los Angeles stood on edge, and its people stood together.

As the lead spokesperson for the Los Angeles Fire Department during that harrowing time, I was tasked with delivering updates to the public—critical safety information, facts, figures, containment percentages. But behind the microphones and press briefings, I bore witness to something far more profound: extraordinary acts of courage, leadership, and humanity that rarely make the headlines.

Written independently on my own time and self-funded, this non-political book is a tapestry of those experiences. It weaves together firsthand accounts from firefighters battling walls of flame, air crews navigating smoke-choked skies, and community members who opened their homes, hearts, and hands to help neighbors in need. It captures the quiet moments of resolve, the split-second decisions that saved lives, and highlights how calm leadership and

Erik Scott

steady voices guided a city through its darkest hours.

Within these pages, you'll find not only a chronicle of the fire itself, but also a reflection on the principles of leadership under pressure—clarity in communication, empathy in action, and the power of trust in turbulent times.

Whether you serve on the front lines of emergency response, guide a team through periods of uncertainty, or strive to understand what it means to lead with purpose, I hope the leadership principles in these pages resonate far beyond the realm of firefighting.

I invite you to walk this road with us. May these stories remind you that resilience is not just a trait—it's a choice, made moment by moment, often in the face of unimaginable odds.

~ Erik Scott

Prologue

THE NIGHT EVERYTHING CHANGED

Tuesday, January 7, 2025 — Pacific Palisades, Los Angeles.

The Palisades Fire did not sleep that first night—and neither did we.

By dusk, neighborhoods glowed orange, streetlights washed out by flames. Evacuations continued, headlights crawled down canyon roads toward Pacific Coast Highway. Police officers went door to door. Firefighters guided families out by flashlight. Buses carried residents from senior facilities. Panic was there, but so was order. Thousands got out safely.

At Will Rogers State Beach, our Incident Command Post (ICP) was under constant pressure. Winds drove embers across the lot, ash coating every surface. Even inside the trailers, smoke hung in the air. At one point, I turned to the team and said, "If we weren't in this trailer, the wind might take it." That wasn't hyperbole—the gusts were so violent it felt like only our weight kept the command post planted. Still, the work didn't stop. Crews checked in. Assignments were issued. Maps updated. Logistics kept food and fuel moving. Operations pushed resources where they were needed most.

On the line, the fire behaved like a serpent of flame spewing

Erik Scott

destruction into the dark. It chewed through canyons, leapt ridges, and threw embers miles ahead. Crews knew they couldn't stop the front head-on—but they could fight it strategically. Tactical patrols became lifelines, leapfrogging into neighborhoods, stamping out spot fires before they claimed entire blocks.

In Marquez Knolls, firefighters defended cul-de-sacs while residents walked past them evacuating on foot. In the Highlands, crews shielded condos from flames racing uphill, improvising when some hydrants ran dry. In Temescal Canyon, strike teams anchored defense in driveways as winds roared through. What might have looked like chaos from above was disciplined determination on the ground.

The winds bent physics. Hose streams curved sideways. Water evaporated before it hit the ground. Yet firefighters kept moving. Engines repositioned again and again, headlights cutting through smoke, hose lines stretched across backyards. Crews worked 36 hours without relief, eyes bloodshot, faces streaked with soot, but their focus stayed the same: defend, protect, hold.

Aircraft were grounded for most of the night, but when the winds eased, pilots seized the moment. Helicopters dipped low to drop water where crews were holding the line—every drop buying time. Fixed-wing tankers laid retardant along ridges to reinforce positions, focusing on stopping the fire at natural breaks—the three R's: rivers, ridges, and roads.

Back at the Incident Command Post, my role was to keep the public informed—and calm. Evacuation orders had to be crystal clear. One wrong word and people could drive into danger instead of away from it. We worked shoulder-to-shoulder with LAPD, syncing messaging with the evacuation branch. The goal never changed: clarity. Turn left, not right. Go south, not north. Leave now.

By midnight, the scale was undeniable. My team had been to

many big fires, but the winds that night were relentless—an intensity unlike anything we had experienced before. The fire had already grown past 3,000 acres. By dawn, it had surged beyond 17,000.

That night became our threshold. What began as a brush fire escalated into a battle against nature's fury, testing every protocol, every instinct, and every ounce of resolve. We didn't know then how far it would spread—or how deeply it would change us.

Erik Scott

Part 1

THE FRONTLINE IN ACTION

Chapter 1

THE CALM BEFORE THE FIRE

**"If we can't extinguish a fire within twenty minutes,
it will erupt into hundreds, maybe thousands, of acres."**
~ Team Incident Commander

Tuesday, January 7, 2025.

At 8:00 a.m., my phone lit up for my LAFD Incident Management Team's weekly on-call conference. That morning, we were already leaning forward. The forecast was unforgiving: hot, dry Santa Ana winds barreling in from the northeast, strong enough to turn a single spark into catastrophe. On the line, our team's Incident Commander didn't waste words with his prophetic warning. Within a very short time, that's exactly what happened.

Our team—one of three elite units within The Los Angeles Fire Department—was on rotation that week. Each team brought together specialists from every discipline: Finance tracked resources and costs. Logistics kept food, fuel, and supplies flowing. Operations directed the boots on the ground. Planning looked ahead, mapping where the fire might go next. Command staff included safety, liaison, and—in my case—public information. Together, those parts made the whole.

In the days leading up to that call, conditions were already signaling trouble. The day before, the National Weather Service had issued Red Flag Warnings, and we were pushing that message hard—reminding the public about the City of Los Angeles' Red Flag Parking Restrictions Program. When those restrictions are in effect, parking is prohibited in posted Very High Fire Hazard Severity Zones—narrow roads, sharp curves, and cul-de-sacs where a single vehicle can block emergency access or trap residents during an evacuation. I reminded viewers that more than 1,700 signs are posted citywide and that vehicles left in violation would be towed to keep routes clear for firefighters and fleeing residents.

By the evening of January 6, I knew the next day's weather would dominate local coverage. Assignment editors were already lining up reporters to cover the wind event. So, early on January 7, I took a step I rarely take: I sent out a formal media advisory to roughly 250 outlets and reporters across Los Angeles, letting them know I'd be available for interviews. The goal was simple—to make sure our message led the coverage, that the public saw how the fire department was mobilizing early, and that they needed to do the same.

As LAFD's longest-serving lead Public Information Officer (PIO), I take the job seriously. My work isn't about being on TV—it's about talking through the news media to the public, reaching them with life-saving information. That morning, I directed news outlets to meet near the site of the 2017 Skirball Fire, in west Los Angeles, just off the 405 Freeway. Even in winter, fire can devastate—that was the message I wanted to deliver.

By 7:00 a.m., the first news crews began arriving. We started live shots and recorded interviews with several local stations. Within an hour, the response was growing quickly—enough that I relocated our setup to a larger nearby parking lot to accommodate the increased media presence. It offered room for multiple news vans, better line-of-sight for live interviews, and safer access for news crews working in windy conditions.

By 8:00 a.m., the lot was busy with cameras, reporters, and tripods—a small media hub forming in real time. My team and I moved from one interview to the next, reinforcing our key message: respect the Red Flag conditions, stay vigilant, and be ready to act.

By 10:00 a.m., news vans filled the lot. Mid-interview, a reporter looked up from her phone and said there was a new fire in the Hollywood Hills—the Sunset Fire. For the next half hour, between interviews, I monitored radio traffic while the reporters checked updates coming in from their news desks. Together, we pieced a rough picture of the incident. Crews were moving quickly, aircraft was on scene, and command was reporting progress. It appeared they were getting a decent handle on it.

We decided to stay put and continue interviews from the Skirball lot. The winds were now starting to howl, and our message about preparedness remained the priority. The day was far from over—but for the moment, the Sunset Fire seemed to be under control.

At 10:30 a.m., another call came through: brushfire in Pacific Palisades. Our ears perked up. The first arriving unit immediately requested ten additional engines. That alone told me everything—this one was showing serious potential.

I told the reporters, "We just called for ten more engines. I'm heading down that way. I'll probably see you there." They packed up to follow.

I made a U-turn onto the 405 South and, fortunately, spotted Strike Team 1880C—five brush engines ripping down the freeway. I tucked in behind them. Six rigs in total—lights and sirens blaring—carved a path through traffic.

Erik Scott

Another familiar sight joined our caravan: an old 2005 yellow F350 diesel pickup with a red stripe down the side. Everyone knew that truck. It belonged to Captain II Rich Diede, who headed up our bulldozer operations.

We exited at Sunset Boulevard and wound through Brentwood neighborhoods toward the Palisades. Then I saw it—a massive, dark column of smoke towering above the ridgeline. Immense. Ominous. I knew instantly: we were in for the long haul.

Traffic was already jammed with evacuees—a stark reminder of why early evacuation is critical. We staged first at Fire Station 23 in the Palisades, where I met up with the Operations West Bureau Commander. The familiar rhythm took over. I scanned for the side of a command vehicle—the place where a map of the incident would usually be taped up, at least three feet by three feet, marked with grease pencil lines showing the current fire perimeter, projected path, and evacuation box. That's the heartbeat of an incident: where strategy meets reality.

My role was clear—communicate that map to the public. Tell residents where the fire was, where it was headed, who needed to leave, and how to get out safely.

One lesson from my mentor, Brian Humphrey, echoed in my mind: Tell people what is happening, what we are doing about it, and what it means to them. That mantra continually guided me. In the first few minutes of any major incident, information is as critical as water. Clear, timely updates can save lives; confusion can cost them. My focus was to turn operational data into public understanding—translate radio traffic and command briefings into plain language that residents could act on. It wasn't about sound bites or headlines; it was about trust. If people believed the information, they would follow it, and that could make all the difference.

The incident footprint had grown rapidly, already too large

for Fire Station 23. We relocated less than a mile down the road to Gladstones, the beachfront restaurant off Pacific Coast Highway, and established it as our temporary alternate base camp. From there, we had more space to stage vehicles, set up command posts, and coordinate with the media while still maintaining a clear view of the smoke column pushing over the hills.

By then, the winds had intensified. What had started as steady gusts was now surging in violent bursts, like a strong bully pushing people around. And for the first time, ash was in the air—drifting, swirling, carried low across the coast. Sand whipped sideways through the parking lot as the sky turned a deeper, smoky gray. You could taste the grit, feel it sticking to your face. Breathing grew harder. Eyes stung, throats burned. One by one, masks started to come on. The sound of the wind mixed with sirens and rotor wash, a constant reminder that the day was only getting worse.

That's also when my team started arriving. Captain Adam Van Gerpen, a former Marine, brought discipline, precision, and a can-do attitude. Firefighter and Public Information Officer David Ortiz, trusted by Los Angeles' Spanish-language media, carried an enormous load—making sure life-saving information reached one of the city's largest communities. Margaret Stewart—sharp, decisive, and already on duty near the 911 Dispatch Center—brought instincts honed as a former U.S. Army Blackhawk pilot and an unmatched ability to track information across multiple channels at once.

From the start, we knew LAFD couldn't shoulder this alone. CAL FIRE Incident Management Team 2, led by Captain Thomas Shoots—who struck that rare balance of humility and competence—arrived on Day One, bringing depth and resources that proved invaluable. Together, we built out a robust Public Information Section. Because the fire was burning inside Los Angeles city

Erik Scott

limits—our terrain, our community, our reporters—I assumed the role of Media Division lead. CAL FIRE brought scale; we brought local knowledge. That blend strengthened us both.

Meanwhile, firefighters across the Palisades were in the fight of their lives. Winds strong enough to rip helmets from heads and shove hose streams sideways. Engines maneuvered through clogged canyon roads. Bulldozers cleared escape lanes. Where hydrants sputtered, firefighters drafted water from swimming pools. Tactical patrols moved block by block, stamping out embers before they could claim entire subdivisions.

For a time, helicopters redirected from the Sunset Fire gave us an edge. But as the winds worsened, that advantage disappeared. Pilots described flying as being tossed in a VW Beetle on a roller coaster, dropping multiple stories in an instant. Their drops shredded mid-air, evaporating before touching the ground. Our shield was down.

We began the morning staging at Fire Station 23, then shifted to Gladstones as the fire accelerated. But as the incident grew and our footprint expanded, we moved to our predetermined basecamp site at Will Rogers State Beach—large, wide, paved parking lots built for staging resources and establishing a full command post.

By nightfall at Will Rogers, the scale of the fire was undeniable. The most accurate description was a hurricane made of fire. Embers blasted in every direction—glowing red against the black sky, stinging like sparks from a grinder. Even with goggles and a cinched-down helmet, I had to hold it in place—otherwise the wind gusts would have ripped it right off my head.

It was now left to the ground crews—and to the words we pushed out to the public: evacuations, escape routes, life-saving guidance. Day One had ended, but the fight was only beginning.

Chapter 2

INTO THE INFERNO

"If the winds hit like I think they will, you'll have
less than an hour to pivot."
~ *Richard Thompson, Meteorologist, National Weather Center*

H e said it two days before the fire broke out. At the time, it
sounded like a worst-case scenario. But by midnight on the
first night, it was our reality. The fire had already grown past 3,000
acres. By dawn, it had surged beyond 17,000. What followed wasn't
just a response—it was a test of every system we had in place.

By the time the first 911 call came in from the Palisades foothills, the winds were already making their presence felt.

At the Will Rogers State Beach Incident Command Post, can-
opies and equipment shelters flexed hard under steady gusts, radios crackled with static, and fine sand ripped through the lot and
across the pavement.

Every forecast model had pointed to this moment—and Richard Thompson had been one of the first to warn us.

Richard had spent nearly three decades with the National
Weather Service (NWS), a calm, precise voice in every storm. To
firefighters, he was simply "Rich," the meteorologist who could

read the sky like a tactical map.

In the days leading up to the fire, he had warned of a "Particularly Dangerous Situation," a PDS—a phrase so rarely used it made even the most seasoned incident commanders pause, and it instantly changed the way firefighters prepare.

It was a perfect alignment of conditions: strong Santa Ana winds, eight months without rain, vegetation still at late-summer dryness, and a mountain-wave pattern that would turn canyons into wind tunnels.

Richard Thompson had seen nearly everything in thirty years of forecasting Southern California weather. Since joining the National Weather Service in 1995, he had been the steady voice behind countless red-flag warnings and winter-storm alerts—a man who translated atmospheric chaos into calm, usable data. But when the first models began showing the January 7 wind event, even he felt unease creeping in.

"I've been an incident meteorologist since 2006," he told me. "I've been on eighty-four major incidents—fires, oil spills, recovery operations—but this one ranks number two for me, just behind the Thomas Fire and the Montecito debris flow. It was that significant."

Over the years, I'd worked with Rich on multiple disasters. Each time he joined our morning briefings, his voice carried weight. An "IMET," as we called them, Incident Meteorologists, was part scientist, part field responder— embedded with the Incident Management Team to provide real-time, on-site forecasts that could guide tactics and protect lives.

A few days before the fire, his team began noticing troubling patterns. Around New Year's, the models hinted at a major Santa Ana event—one strong enough to warrant the highest alert level.

"As the days wore on—January 1, 2, 3—it just kept looking worse," he said. "Stronger, drier, more widespread. So we started messaging early—emails, webinars, and daily calls with fire agencies—LA City, LA County, Ventura, the Forest Service. Everyone needed to be ready."

By January 5, the Weather Service upgraded to a Red Flag Warning, which signals that wind, heat, and low humidity could lead to extreme fire behavior. That warning, combined with the rare PDS tag, is only used when meteorologists believe life-threatening conditions are imminent.

Typical triggers:
- Sustained winds > 25 mph or gusts > 60 mph
- Relative humidity < 15 % for six hours or more
- Critically dry vegetation and fuels
- High confidence across multiple forecast models

In Southern California, a PDS Red Flag Warning may appear only once every five to ten years—unless, as in January 2025, months of drought turn the improbable into reality.

For firefighters, seeing PDS flash across a weather bulletin means one thing: whatever wildfire contingency plans you had, double them; whatever margin you thought you had, cut it in half.

Normally, the strongest Santa Anas arrive mid-winter—after rain has dampened the fuels. Not this year.

"We hadn't had measurable rain since the previous spring," Rich said. "Eight or nine months dry. Vegetation was still at late-summer levels. When those Santa Anas hit, it was like striking a match over tinder."

Compounding it all was a phenomenon that few outside meteorology circles understand—mountain waves—oscillating bursts of wind that tumble down slopes, briefly intensifying surface gusts. "Think of them as multipliers," he explained. "The Santa Anas alone were bad enough, but the mountain-wave setup pushed it over the edge. Some gusts topped 80 miles per hour."

Erik Scott

By dawn on January 7, the ingredients had combined. Thompson was at his desk in Oxnard, scanning the Alert Wildfire cameras, when smoke appeared over the Palisades.

"I looked up and saw it—the foothills lighting up," he said. "You could tell right away the winds were going to drive it hard. Honestly, I thought, 'Yeah, I'll probably be going to that one.' Sure enough, the next day I got the call."

For the next fourteen days, Thompson embedded at the Incident Command Post, working long shifts alongside fireline crews and command staff.

"By 5:00 a.m., I'd be up, checking wind speeds, humidity, temperature drops. 6:30 a.m., pre-op briefings; 7:00 a.m., briefing the crews heading to the line. Planning meetings, coordination calls—it's nonstop. But it's what we train for," Thompson said.

Years of professional detachment couldn't blunt the impact—the devastation still shook him.

"As meteorologists, we have to compartmentalize," he said. "But seeing the destruction—homes gone, lives upended—it hit me. I couldn't bring myself to tour the burn area afterward. I still haven't. You know what's there, and you wish so badly you were wrong."

He paused. "That's the hardest part of this job—knowing you forecasted it perfectly."

We talked about the paradox we both feel—the mix of adrenaline and sorrow.

"People see meteorologists get animated during big events," he said. "They think, 'Why are they excited about something so destructive?' It's not excitement for tragedy—it's engagement in your craft. You're trained for this. You want to perform at your best when it matters most."

I told him it's no different for firefighters. Your training, instinct, and focus all converge. You're not eager for destruction—you're ready to help.

Before we ended, I asked what he hoped people would take away from this event.

"I just hope people remember how extreme this was," he said. "The winds, the dryness, the timing—it was the perfect storm. But there are lessons in it for all of us: meteorologists, firefighters, the community. We can always improve how we message, how we prepare, how we respond. I hope this fire isn't forgotten—I hope it's studied."

He smiled faintly, the analytical calm returning. "It was catastrophic, yes. But it was also a learning event. And that's how we get better—all of us."

~~~~~

By late morning on January 7, his forecast was no longer theoretical—it was unfolding.

The wind tore through Mandeville and Marquez Knolls, bending hose streams before they reached the flame front. Aircraft tried to make drops, but turbulence forced them back.

This was the PDS event Thompson warned about—the particularly dangerous situation no one ever wants to see verified in real time.

The forecast had become reality, moving across canyons faster than we could react. Radio traffic blended into a constant stream—structure protection, evacuations, requests for aircraft that couldn't launch. The air was dry enough to sting, every gust carrying static.

We weren't fighting a fire anymore. We were matching pace with the atmosphere.

The winds continued through the night, with gusts exceed-

Erik Scott

ing 80 miles per hour in some canyons and reports of even stronger bursts along the ridgelines. Thompson's forecast had been exact—every parameter he warned of had materialized. For us on the ground, it confirmed what we already knew: the weather would dictate everything that followed.

~~~~~

At Fire Station 69 in the Palisades, Captain Jeff Brown was living that reality with his crew. With 36 years on the job, he had seen earthquakes, riots, and countless brush fires, but he later admitted, "Nothing compares to the scale of this incident."

That morning, before the first plume rose, Brown had reminded his firefighters to stay sharp. Hours later, they were pushing up Palisades Drive, heading toward the Highlands where the fire first took hold. For much of the day, they fought deep in the neighborhood, carving out a stand that, for a time, held the flames at bay. When they were reassigned, every home in their sector still stood.

By late afternoon, around 4:00 p.m., Brown and his crew were redeployed to El Medio. There was no pause, no easing into the fight—they were injected straight into an immediate battle.

But as night fell, the winds changed violently. Gusts doubled and then tripled, some strong enough to rip shingles from roofs. What had felt like a tactical victory unraveled in hours. The same homes they had spent the day defending—many belonging to families they knew personally—were destroyed as ember storms swept the hillsides. By sunrise, nearly the entire neighborhood had burned, including the home of a couple in their nineties who had lived there for more than sixty years.

Brown's firefighters had fought with little more than grit. Even with goggles strapped on, their eyes burned, and their faces showed the battle. "Normally, ten companies fight one house fire," Brown explained. "Here, thousands of homes stood threatened with barely fifty companies. It was overwhelming."

And yet, what struck him most was not fear, but pride. Off-duty members reported in to defend the firehouse itself. Crews improvised, "Their attitude was, what can we do with minimum resources to protect this community?" Brown said. "Our little success became very big—and we still hang our hat on that."

Later, when the adrenaline wore off, his wife asked him a question that stopped him cold. Had he feared for his life? For the first time in his career, he hesitated before answering. "I told her no, I wasn't fearful—but I hesitated," he admitted. That pause told its own story. The fire, the heat, the endless ember cast—it was unlike anything he had faced before. He recalled the sheer force of it: beach volleyball nets a quarter mile away, warping from the radiant heat, as if the fire itself had rewritten the laws of nature.

Brown drew strength from his family's legacy. Firefighting ran deep—his father, brothers, and now his son all wore the badge. "We have it in our blood to work hard, put the community first, and do everything we can short of giving our lives," he said. That sense of heritage gave him resolve, and his crew carried that same grit into the night.

~~~~~

This wasn't the first time the Palisades had burned. I'd responded to the Pacific Palisades before—once in 2019, when a brush fire scorched forty-two acres, and again in 2021, when another blaze grew past 1,200 acres and forced days of evacuations.

Familiar, recurring wildfire hazards reemerged—narrow roads that could trap evacuees, steep canyons that funneled fire

Erik Scott

uphill, and ember-driven runs that tested neighborhoods block by block. We adapted with every deployment, refining our tactics each time, but by 2025, when flames surged beyond 17,000 acres in less than forty-eight hours, those challenges evolved too—returning at a scale none of us had faced before, or could have imagined.

This quickly became a story of endurance, integrity, and courage—crews pushing through 36 hours without relief or adequate rest, finding ways to fight even when water sources ran dry, and engines holding their ground in cul-de-sacs as flames swept past. A strike team captain positioned his rigs just right. A firefighter kicked in a door to pull a trapped resident. A pilot braved turbulence to make a decisive drop. Each of these things happened. Each act mattered. Each act saved lives.

By the time the 2025 Palisades Fire was only beginning to reveal its full scope, it had already made one thing clear: even in the face of extreme fire behavior, we would not break. We would adapt, fight, and hold the line as best we could. We were not about to give up.

Chapter 3

THE HORN IN THE DARK

"… words cannot describe the way I was feeling as I sat in my car with the hills burning around me, thinking I was going to die… I looked up and saw the lights of your truck heading toward me and realized my savior had come to rescue me."

~ Patty Sarantinos

January 7–10, 2025 — Pacific Palisades/Big Rock, Malibu.

By late afternoon, the sky over Big Rock—an oceanside enclave of homes along Pacific Coast Highway, just west of the Getty Villa—had taken on the color of rusted metal, smoke staining the light until even the sun looked foreign. From a turnout overlooking three ridgelines, James Sarantinos watched the glowing smoke column advance ridge to ridge, then accelerate. Earlier that day, the wind had driven the fire toward the coastline, and he—like many—believed it would stop there. "Everybody was kind of thinking it's going to burn itself out… pretty much at the coastline," he later said.

Near dusk, the wind shifted and slammed into Big Rock. What had seemed distant became immediate. James drove the quarter mile back up Seaboard Road and stepped inside. "Look—we've got to go. It's here," he told his wife, Patty.

They had rehearsed this moment: two cars to split the risk, meet where the road widened near the Mesa, then head for safety at the Pacific Coast Highway (PCH). The power had failed, but their generator kept the television alive with a constant flow of updates. Months earlier, Patty had rescued a stray cat for her elderly neighbor, Meredith Heron, naming it Socks. The simple act of saving that cat would ultimately help save her own life.

When the fire came, Meredith's sons—Rick and Mike—returned to help their mother find Socks before evacuating. The cat was terrified, hiding deep inside the house, and it took nearly thirty minutes to coax her out. That delay changed everything.

By the time the brothers began driving down Seaboard Road, propane tanks were exploding like artillery, and the air was filled with burning debris. "It was like bombs going off," Patty recalled. As Rick and Mike turned onto Big Rock Drive, they heard a car horn blaring somewhere above them but couldn't see through the smoke. They assumed it was another vehicle burning.

When they finally reached Pacific Coast Highway, they found James desperately searching for Patty—frantic, covered in ash, asking every firefighter he could find for help. "Did you see her?" he pleaded.

The brothers looked at each other and realized what they'd heard. "Oh my God," one of them said. "That was her."

They told James exactly where they'd heard the horn echoing through the canyon. That critical detail—born of a half-hour delay to save a cat—provided the clue they needed to find Patty's car.

Unbeknownst to her, that desperate blast of the horn—and a frightened cat named Socks—had just changed the course of the night.

As the wind roared and the hills above Big Rock ignited, Patty and James began their escape plan. Koda, their Australian Shepherd, rode up front with Patty. James followed behind in a separate vehicle, each of them believing they would meet again safely at the bottom.

As Patty descended toward PCH, the world disappeared. Smoke and embers filled the air like a blizzard of fire. She described it as "vertigo, but with flames." Somewhere in that swirl, her tires rolled onto a narrow dirt spur—a side road climbing above Big Rock. She never saw it. When she pressed the brake, the car skidded, then lurched and stopped, high-centered on a boulder that wedged beneath the rear axle.

Unbeknownst to her at the time, that rock kept the vehicle from sliding off the unseen drop behind her. But in the moment, it only meant one thing—she was stuck. In the middle of fleeing for her life, the car that was supposed to carry her to safety had become a trap. Heat pressed through the glass, the air thick with smoke, and flames flickered in every mirror.

Koda whimpered from the passenger seat as she threw the car into reverse again, the tires spinning uselessly. For the first time, she realized she couldn't move—not forward, not backward—and the fire was closing in.

She cracked the door to look, and wind hurled embers inside. Koda crawled onto her lap, trembling. She dialed 911. The call reached the LA County Sheriff's Department Lost Hills Station, where Dispatcher Harrison Knowles answered.

"I was panicking," she later said. "He told me I had to calm down so he could help me." They tried everything, but the car wouldn't budge. The line transferred again, then went dead. Knowles had told her that if she lost connection, she should lay on the horn so rescuers could find her.

So she did.

Erik Scott

"I was praying to God to let me die from smoke inhalation," she told me. "Please don't let me be burned alive."

Down below, James reached PCH—but Patty wasn't there. The hillside above him roared like a freight train. Intense dry heat rolled off the canyon walls in waves, and the wind drove embers across the highway like horizontal rain. "Fourteen homes on fire... within fifteen minutes," he said. Roofs and decks were already collapsing in the gusts, sending burning debris tumbling into the road. Power lines draped across the pavement like tripwires; some still live and sparking. Rockslides and blown transformers cracked in the wind.

Every few seconds, another explosion echoed up the canyon. Visibility was quickly diminishing—a swirl of smoke, flame, and hurricane-force gusts. James moved through the chaos, scanning for Patty's headlights, then circled back uphill, unwilling to leave without knowing if she'd made it out.

On PCH near the base of Big Rock, he began pleading with firefighters for help. His face, Patty would recall later, was gray with ash and terror, but steady eyes locked on anyone who might listen. The fire front was just beginning to blow through the area, and most engines were already engaged in rescues and structure defense. Downed telephone poles blocked access, and the flame front had already swept over the roadway once. The large heavy fire engines found the sharp turn up Big Rock difficult to navigate, especially in those winds, and crews feared the wind would blow the fire back over them. Rough roads like Patty's were even less accessible.

That's when James met Captain Malcolm Dicks of the Los Angeles County Fire Department, a 25-year veteran with five more in San José before that. Dicks had just finished loading a seventy-year-old homeowner into his pickup—a man who'd been thrown a hundred feet by hurricane-force gusts while trying to defend his house with a garden hose. His leg was badly broken—twisted in a way that made it clear he needed to get out fast— and the responding squad couldn't reach him after blowing a tire on a fallen pole along the narrow approach. So Dicks loaded him up and drove him out himself.

When James approached, desperate, Dicks listened.

"My wife is up there," James said. "She's trapped."

"Let's try," Dicks replied. "You're coming with me."

They climbed into Captain Dicks's four-wheel-drive pick-up—a Ford F-150, far smaller and more maneuverable than the engines below—and began threading their way up the burning canyon. The narrow road twisted between downed poles and flaming debris, the truck's tires crunching over shattered glass and embers. The wind kept rearranging the problem as they moved—branches falling, wires snapping, new fires crossing the road behind them. At one bend, they passed a brand-new truck half-hanging off the shoulder, its driver overcome by smoke and gone on foot. "She should be somewhere around here," James kept saying.

Visibility was now near zero. The air roared with heat and wind. Everything around them glowed red—flames, embers, even the smoke itself. In that crimson haze, red taillights vanished completely. Then, through the smoke, Dicks caught a flash of bright white light. It was the car's reverse lamps—the only light that could pierce through the red glow of the firestorm. "That's the only reason I saw it," he later said.

They stopped and jumped out, sprinting uphill roughly a hundred yards through the gusting inferno. The wind hammered at their faces, and embers blew sideways like burning sand. Dicks led the way, his turnout jacket hissing as embers stuck and burned onto the fabric. The roar of the wind and fire drowned out every-

Erik Scott

thing else.

At the top of the rise, they found her. Patty had been trapped twenty to thirty minutes, her car half off the narrow dirt spur, smoke filling the interior. Koda was pressed against her, trembling. She saw movement through the haze and began shouting for help. "Please save me," she cried as Dicks reached her door.

He pulled the handle and yanked it open. Heat poured out. "You're not safe yet," he told her firmly, his voice cutting through the wind. He guided her out of the vehicle, steadying her as her legs gave out from exhaustion and smoke inhalation. Behind them, the car's paint was already blistering.

Koda followed close, and James quickly grabbed the dog's leash as they started moving downhill. The pavement was blistering from radiant heat, but in the chaos they kept moving, unaware that Koda's paws had been burned. Dicks lifted the seventy-pound Australian Shepherd into his arms while keeping his other hand on Patty's shoulder to guide her through the smoke. "We've got you," he said. "Keep moving—we still have to drive out of this."

They stumbled through the swirling smoke back toward the F-150, trying not to slip on ash and debris. When they reached the truck, its paint was partially melted from radiant heat, the windshield streaked with soot. Dicks helped Patty and Koda inside, slammed the doors shut, and took one last look uphill—everything above them was burning.

As they started back down, the descent proved even more harrowing than the climb. The wind shifted violently, pushing tongues of flame across the road in front of them. Burning branches fell from the canyon walls, and the smoke was so dense Dicks could see only a few feet ahead. He crept forward in four-wheel drive, weaving between downed power lines and fallen telephone poles that littered the narrow road. Every turn revealed something new—glowing embers, half-collapsed fences, cars abandoned mid-escape.

"We didn't know if we'd make it back out," he recalled. The world had become a moving obstacle course of fire.

When they reached the bottom, the line of fire had shifted again. The place they'd come from was now burning. Dicks kept Patty and Koda in his truck and told James to follow in his vehicle. "You have to go north," he said. "South is impassable."

The small convoy crawled through flame and debris toward Fire Station 70 on Carbon Canyon Road. The wind drove the fire across Pacific Coast Highway in bursts, and as they approached, Dicks could see roofs burning on both sides of the street. Inside the station, alarms blared and power flickered as evacuees huddled on the floor—families, pets, even a few firefighters who had been overcome by smoke. Crews were setting up makeshift triage inside the apparatus bay, treating the injured and exhausted as calls poured in faster than anyone could answer them.

Dicks handed Patty, James, and Koda over to station personnel.

"What's your name?" Patty asked.

"Malcolm," he said.

Patty thanked him through tears. She learned he was from Pacoima and had only just arrived from another rescue before finding her. "He risked his life to save mine," she later told me.

The fire station was still under threat, alarms blaring as crews scrambled to protect nearby homes. Dicks gave a quick nod to the family, then turned back toward his truck. The fire was still advancing. Moments later, he was gone again—back into the smoke.

Outside, the wind howled through the canyon. The three of them—Patty, James, and Koda—sat together in the station, faces streaked with soot, the dog still trembling. Around them, radios crackled with new calls, and the air smelled of wet ash and diesel.

Erik Scott

For the first time in hours, they were safe, though the night was far from over.

By the time the winds began to ease, the fire had already carved its path through Big Rock and the neighboring canyons. In Santa Barbara, 73 miles away, their son Devin had spent hours calling and refreshing evacuation maps, unable to reach them. When the call finally went through late that night, he learned his parents were alive—tired, shaken, and sheltering with friends on the lake in Westlake Village. It was a small calm in the chaos, the first steady breath after a night that had seemed endless.

The next day, James and Devin returned by back roads to check on the house. The sky was still orange, the air sharp with ash. "A weird miracle," Devin said. Many of the houses nearby were gone; theirs still stood. "By the grace of God," James whispered.

For the next several days, father and son worked the ruins, stamping out hot spots with shovels and water jugs a neighbor had stockpiled. Devin doused a hedge that had reignited along the property line, pulled up smoking railroad ties, and made a list of which homes had burned and which had survived. Tragically, two of their neighbors in Big Rock had not made it out.

In the weeks that followed, Patty located Los Angeles County Sheriff's Department 911 Dispatcher Harrison Knowles to thank him for his steady voice on the phone that night. She also insisted on publicly honoring Captain Dicks for his extraordinary courage. CBS2 / KCAL9 reporter Michelle Gile helped Patty and James reconnect with both men, setting the stage for their reunion.

I remember being at the command post at Will Rogers State Beach when word of the rescue first reached our team. A few of my PIOs told me what had happened up Big Rock, and it stopped us in our tracks. I spoke with LA County Fire PIO Sheila Kelleher and told her to run with the story—it was their member's heroism, and the public needed to know what he'd done.

At County Fire Station 70, Fire Chief Anthony Marrone and Supervisor Lindsey Horvath joined Patty for a small ceremony covered by Gile. Patty read aloud the letter she had written:

"Dear Malcolm, words cannot describe the way I was feeling as I sat in my car with the hills burning around me, thinking I was going to die. As I sat there with my dog Koda, thinking it was over, I looked up and saw the lights of your truck heading toward me and realized my savior had come to rescue me."

Afterward, Patty arranged for the massive boulder—the same one that stopped her car from sliding off the hillside—to be moved to the front of their property. She hired a backhoe to lift it from its original spot and deliver it to her yard, where it now sits as a permanent reminder of that night. A bronze plaque rests on it, engraved:

"God saved my life with a miracle on 1-7-2025 in the form of this boulder, with the help of Fire Capt. Malcolm, a cat named Socks, my beloved husband James, and our dog Koda."

The reunion and ceremony were deeply emotional, but true to his nature, Captain Dicks downplayed any notion of heroism. He spoke quietly afterward, standing just outside the bay doors of Station 70, looking out toward the blackened hills that still carried smoke. For him, the rescue wasn't about recognition—it was about responsibility, the part of the job that never quite leaves you.

"We're used to winning," Dicks said later. "And you keep losing. You get back up and go to the next home, the next street, the next community."

That line stayed with me. It resonated with countless firefighters across agencies who, in the heat of the battle, were being pummeled by conditions unlike anything we'd faced before. We're accustomed to having a full assignment—engines, trucks, and

Erik Scott

crews—focused on a single house fire. During the Palisades Fire, the winds were so extreme, the fire so relentless, that we kept losing despite our best efforts. That was hard then, and it's still hard now. But as Dicks said, you keep going—to the next home, the next street, the next community.

That quote also struck a chord with the next generation—Patty and James's son, Devin. Learning his mother narrowly escaped and seeing the courage of Captain Dicks left an indelible mark on him. What happened in Big Rock didn't just change his family's life; it changed his direction in life.

When I later spoke with him, he said the experience gave him clarity and purpose. "It was a cataclysmic shift," he told me. "I wanted direct impact in my community." Within months, he completed a five-week firefighter training program in Wyoming, a three-day course in Lompoc, earned his First Responder and EMT certifications, and registered for the Monterey Park Fire Academy. His goal: join a Santa Barbara County crew, gain wildland experience, and one day test for a large municipal fire department.

I told him we'd be here to help him along the way—that's how the fire service works. Every firefighter has been lifted by others at some point in their career, and we take pride in paying that forward. Devin's path is still being written, *but his fire was lit on that night in January.*

Chapter 4

THE SKY ABOVE THE FIRE

"I've seen devastation on the ground—Santa Rosa, Napa—but
from the air, all at once, it was overwhelming."
~ *Battalion Chief Brett Willis*

On January 7, the sky over Los Angeles turned into a chessboard.
Thirty minutes before the Palisades ignition, Air Ops was already spinning up for the Sunset Fire in Hollywood. The President was in town, and a Presidential Temporary Flight Restriction—a 30-mile "POTUS TFR" ring that's standard whenever the President or Vice President is in town—meant a quick but standard call to the Secret Service and air traffic control before lifting off.

"Anytime we have overlapping incidents, it challenges us," Battalion Chief Brett Willis said. "But that day it helped: we were already airborne for the Sunset Fire in Hollywood, which is the only reason we could reach Palisades so fast."

The sequence was clinical and fast. Ground crews at the Sunset Fire requested Air Ops; Willis' team got the clearance and a transponder code and launched. En route, Captain II Brandon Rudy—flying the HELCO ship (HELCO = helicopter coordinator, the aerial supervisor for helicopters)—looked right and saw a smoke column over the Palisades. He called the Sunset Fire Incident Commander: a higher-priority fire was building—what did they still need from aircraft? Minutes later came permission to divert.

By the time the first LAFD helicopter orbited Palisades, it was a single-pilot with water aboard. "He did a quick circle to orient and put the first load down," Willis said. It hit at or just before the first engine companies arrived—only possible because the ships were already in the air.

Within the hour, the layered air picture over the Westside— pilots call it "the stack"—filled in: LA County and Ventura County helicopters, Super Scoopers, fixed-wing air attack, and tankers. "By early afternoon, we had fixed-wing," Willis said. "They dropped somewhere around thirty-five thousand gallons of retardant on Day One." Fixed-wing aircraft operate by day; once darkness falls, the sky belongs to helicopters.

If the ground fight is a street brawl, the airspace is a string quartet on a metronome. From the top: air attack in a fixed-wing doing steady orbits; beneath them, tankers and scoopers; beneath them, HELCO; and at the lowest working band, the water-dropping helicopters around 500 AGL—above ground level. Quick read for skimmers: HELCO draws invisible "fences" (e.g., "west of the ridge = tankers, east = helicopters") and brings every inbound aircraft into the pattern so nobody shares the same sky at the same time.

"We separate altitudes and directions, assign dip and fuel sites, and stagger cycles so five ships don't all peel off for gas at once," Willis said. "We're also the division in the air—eyes for Operations when smoke and distance hide the truth."

From that perch, the truth on January 7 came hard and fast: wind, topography, and low fuel moisture perfectly aligned. Multiple spot fires. Retardant lines challenged and, in places, failing. Homes igniting faster than resources could reach them. "We'd make a 360 and tell the Branch Director, 'twenty minutes to impact.' Next orbit: 'Five minutes to impact.' The fire was growing that fast." Those calls weren't abstract. They pointed to specific neighborhoods— Tuna Canyon racing toward the coast; the Palisades Highlands and Castellammare below; and, later, the risk that Mandeville Canyon could go, and then Brentwood beyond it.

By 7:30 p.m., the radios sounded different. Pilots were calling "going around"—aviation shorthand for breaking off an approach to try again—over and over. Turbulence shoved aircraft up and down without warning. Drops drifted wide or broke into mist before they touched heat. "In low wind, a pilot can be higher and still be precise," Willis said. "That night, the wind took it—right or left—no matter the technique. Even shifting a few rotor-widths upwind to use drift, the load was gone. For the heavies? Worse. Less maneuverable. They couldn't get low enough in those canyons."

At Malibu's 69-Bravo helispot and weather site, one aircraft reported sustained winds over 60 mph and gusts near 90 mph. The readout matched it. At some point, Dan Child [Chief Pilot] and I looked at each other and asked, "What are we doing here?" The answer was: "We're done."

Around 7:45 p.m., with severe turbulence, ineffective drops, growing darkness, and pilots openly uncomfortable, Willis made the call to stop air operations for the night: The response—air and ground—was immediate and unified. "No pushback," he said. "We're firefighters; we want to keep working. But the risk lens has to win. We weren't going to ball one up on a hillside."

It wasn't a guess. Air Ops had been training for these decisions for years—with formal safety programs, a culture that encourages candid hazard reports, and post-incident debriefs that turn lessons into procedure. That culture was forged in tragedy.

Erik Scott

In 1998, a Los Angeles Fire Department helicopter crashed near Griffith Park while transporting a critically injured child, killing all three crew members and the patient. The accident was caused by a catastrophic tail rotor failure, marking one of the department's most tragic losses.

That crash has always resonated deeply with me. Early in my career, one of my field assignments was at the old Fire Station 81 in the San Fernando Valley—the station where Firefighter/Paramedics Eric F. Reiner and Michael A. Butler, both from 81-B, were last assigned before the 1998 tragedy. In the early 2000s, during the department's reorganization, the house transitioned to Fire Station 7, but the memory of that loss stayed rooted in the walls. We hung a plaque there honoring them, and every time I walked past it, I felt the weight of what their sacrifice meant. That history is part of why the decisions made in the air on January 7 carried such gravity.

The line from the 1998 fatal crash to now is straight: fly the mission, survive the mission. "We slept fine with that call," Willis said. "It was the right decision."

From the air on the night of January 7, Willis saw perfect squares of flame and asked a pilot what they were. He knew—he just needed a moment to accept it—they were rows of homes burning. It was overwhelming.

~~~~~

January 8. The winds peaked around 2:00 a.m. and backed off. At first light, the carousel started again. Quick swaps kept ships turning—land at Van Nuys, fresh pilot in, refuel, relaunch. Maintenance inspectors worked overnight so helicopters weren't grounded for scheduled checks. Helicopter companies Leonardo and Bell both called to pledge mechanics and parts; none were needed. No component failures. No grounded aircraft. The system held.

For the pilots themselves, those decisions weren't abstract—they lived in the cockpit. One of them was Jonith Johnson, who was recalled to the Palisades Fire just after returning from a leadership training convention. "It was all hands on deck," he recalled. "We called back every pilot so we could keep the helicopters flying around the clock with fresh crews. Fatigue management is critical—in a helicopter, one tired mistake can be fatal."

Johnson joined the response on the second night of the fire. "It was pretty daunting," he said. "This incident encompassed every bit of training and skill we had—decision-making, managing fatigue, dealing with extreme conditions." During the initial attack, pilots sometimes flew for six straight hours before they could rotate out. After that, the schedule settled into a demanding rhythm: four hours in the air, eight hours down. Crews swapped out continuously, so the helicopters rarely sat idle. Even then, exhaustion was a constant threat.

What made the mission especially dangerous were the incredible winds and thick smoke. "Some nights, you'd be flying through violent gusts that shook the aircraft. Other times, you couldn't see anything because of the smoke. On top of that, it was dark, and we were on night vision goggles. It's like looking through toilet paper tubes on a two-dimensional screen. You have to slow down, stay disciplined, and not let the intensity push you into making a bad move."

The first night of the fire, Johnson wasn't yet on duty—but his fellow pilots shared what they had endured. "They said the winds were so violent they'd never felt anything like it. Water drops weren't even effective; the wind just blew them away. The right call was to land the aircraft. You never want to add to the incident by pushing beyond what's safe."

Erik Scott

Helicopter operations are tightly linked to ground crews. "Every major fire has a HELCO—a helicopter coordinator," Johnson explained. "They're the bridge between the Incident Command and the aircraft, directing priorities and drops. Sometimes, ground supervisors will signal us directly, even using mirrors in the daytime to pinpoint targets. At night, the HELCO can use lasers to guide drops with precision. After each drop, they'll give feedback: did we hit the mark, or do we need to adjust? You never hit every shot perfectly. Conditions are always shifting. But you use the last drop to guide the next one."

One of Johnson's strongest memories was making a decision in mid-flight that he felt made a real difference. "There was one house—the homeowner was in the backyard with a garden hose, and the flames were already against the walls. Another pilot and I decided to team up, alternating drops right on that spot. We lost one nearby house, but we saved his and probably the neighbors'. The next day, we flew over again, and the house was still standing. I'll never forget the look on that homeowner's face."

But not every battle could be won. "The hardest part is when embers get into the attic or through a window," Johnson explained. "We're fighting the flame front on the mountainside, trying to stop it from reaching the homes, but the ember cast can still penetrate. Once fire is inside a house, there's not much we can do. That's when you have to move on to protect what you still can."

It's in those moments that the operation depends on teamwork—strike teams, hand crews, and dozers working in unison, reading each other's moves without words, every decision focused on saving what still stood.

For Johnson, the experience was deeply personal. "We don't do this job for recognition, though we got plenty after the fire. The real impact was seeing people who lost everything. That could've been me—my own house is in a fire-prone area just 30 minutes away. You wish you could save everyone, but that's not reality. That's the hardest part to live with."

As the days wore on, new fires erupted across Southern California—the Eaton, Lydia, Kenneth, and Hughes among them—tearing through the foothills, valleys, and canyons from the city to the county line. It wasn't just one incident anymore; it was a regional firestorm, stretching every agency and aircraft to the limit. Camarillo became the primary helibase, but it sat in a notorious wind corridor, forcing Air Operations to stage additional aircraft in Santa Maria, Lancaster, and Santa Monica to keep them flyable and ready to launch as conditions allowed. LA's airspace added its own complexity with multiple airports—Van Nuys, Burbank, Whiteman, Santa Monica, and LAX traffic all had to be threaded while we fought a city-sized fire.

~~~~~

When winds eased, air crews moved fast. Helicopters dropped water into canyons where ground crews were holding. Fixed-wing tankers painted retardant lines along ridges to slow the advance. But the air war wasn't without setbacks—one of the Quebec 1 "Super Scoopers" was struck by a civilian drone. Maintenance crews later discovered a 3-inch by 6-inch hole in the wing from the impact, causing the plane to be grounded during critical operations.

During the Palisades Fire, we repeatedly warned that unauthorized drones in fire airspace could delay or ground aerial firefighting. The FAA reminded the public that this interference is a federal crime, subject to civil fines up to $75,000 and even jail time. In this case, the drone strike grounded a rare and specialized aircraft—one of only two operational water-scooping planes—and

Erik Scott

gave the fire precious time to spread. The plane landed safely, but it was out of service for two of the most intense days of the firefight.

That reckless choice had consequences long after the fire. The drone operator was later convicted in federal court, sentenced to a short prison term, and placed on home detention with community service. He was also ordered to pay more than $150,000 in fines and restitution, including over $65,000 to repair the aircraft.

~~~~~

Friday night, January 10, the wind finally relented. Night operations did "a lot of damage"—the good kind. Willis was watching Mandeville Canyon. "I told the pilot, 'If this wind shifts, we could lose Mandeville.' The wind did shift. Fixed-wing wasn't up yet, so Willis started working the phones himself—Ventura and Orange County ships—building from four night helicopters to thirteen by daybreak. When the tankers finally checked in, helicopters cleared the pattern to give them the lane, and the big planes pounded the line. It was a turning point.

Air alone can't finish it. "We do an awesome job," Willis said. "But we can't put the fire out by ourselves. We support the firefighters on the ground—those digging line, pulling hose, and defending homes."

And still, they worked. Days blurred. Nights bled into mornings. Families waited. "My kids started asking if I live at the hangar now," he said, with a laugh that wasn't quite a laugh. Crews rotated through dark, cold bunkrooms for real rest—and then lifted again. Community support flowed in: meals, notes, and small kindnesses that matter at 3:00 a.m.

Relationships turned into resources at speed. "Who gets to order a helicopter by text?" Willis said, half kidding, half not. That only happens when trust is banked long before the ask. Those relationships—city, county, and state—are why aircraft already overhead the Palisades could be redirected within minutes to knock back the Hughes and Kenneth starts, and why, when we called for help to hold Mandeville, the reply was simply, "On the way."

Looking back, the January 7 shutdown will never be mistaken for retreat. It was proof of a culture that's learned the cost of pushing past the line—and refuses to pay it again. "We're problem solvers," Willis said. "It's in us to keep going. But safety took priority. It was a leadership test, and the right call." By the time CAL FIRE's full team took the reins, LAFD had teed up a clean handoff: helicopters cycling, communications templates set, helibase humming, the TFR paperwork in place, the night program ready. And we stayed in it—especially at night—until the weather and the lines finally gave the city a chance.

"We lost a lot," Willis said. "We saved a lot." The measure wasn't rhetoric. It was neighborhoods still standing at sunrise. It was Mandeville held when the wind blinked. It was a city that, after the worst night, still had a tomorrow."

~~~~~

In May 2017, I was deployed for three days to a stubborn fire in Mandeville Canyon, just east of Pacific Palisades. It burned 55 acres—not massive by wildfire standards—but the location made it one of the most dangerous kinds of fires: steep terrain, one way in and one way out, with multimillion-dollar homes perched above.

I slept in my old silver Crown Victoria on Mountain Gate Drive, grabbing a few hours between shifts. With no logistical camp established, we bedded down where we could and went right back to work. Nearly 300 firefighters labored almost 60 hours to contain

Erik Scott

it, while helicopters hammered hotspots too steep for hand crews.

Investigators later determined the cause was accidental—sparks from metal blades used during brush clearance on a hot, dry afternoon. A well-intentioned act that, under the wrong conditions, became a wildfire.

Mandeville wasn't just a lesson in 2017—it was a preview. The 2017 burn footprint overlapped areas we would battle again in the 2025 Palisades Fire. Standing on those ridgelines years later, stamping out embers in the same terrain, I couldn't help but think: our prevention choices live on far longer than the flames themselves.

Chapter 5

THE IRON LINE

"I had to wear a chin strap just to keep my helmet from blowing off... embers hit me in the throat and went down my shirt."

~ Captain II Richard Diede

The helicopters fought hard, but air alone can't stop a wind-driven wildfire. At some point, the line has to be held from the ground. Bulldozers—massive, slow-moving, but relentless—were carving firebreaks across the Santa Monica Mountains. And leading that effort was someone I've trusted and learned from on countless incidents: Captain II Richard Diede.

Rich is a straight shooter. Before we got into the details of the Palisades Fire, he took a moment to reflect on my role as Public Information Officer.

"You're recognized in the industry, even outside our department, as someone who does the right thing," he told me. "When you're interviewed, the way you tell the story is educated—you never make sh*t up. You're knowledgeable, and if you don't know something, you do your homework. That's what I respect. I support what you're doing 100%."

Coming from Rich, those words carried weight. I've worked numerous incidents with him over the years, and I've come to respect him, learn from him, and consider him a friend. He's the kind of guy you're genuinely glad to bump into on a big, chaotic incident—because you know the work will get done right, you'll pick up something valuable just by being around him, and you'll always share a laugh along the way. Rich balances grit, competence, and humility with a wicked sense of humor.

"I was the strike team leader of the heavy equipment—the dozer unit," he said. "Dozers don't work independently; they operate under a heavy equipment boss. I'm qualified as both a heavy equipment boss and a strike team leader."

In practice, that meant overseeing fire road access in the hills, helipad upkeep, winter drainage repairs, and—when the wind howled—leading our heavy equipment on the fireline. In short, he was in charge of the department's bulldozer strike team.

Because the wind event was predicted, CAL OES (Office of Emergency Services) pre-positioned our Type 1 dozer strike team inside the city. His complement: two Caterpillar D8s—about 93,000 pounds each with 16-foot blades—each on a low-boy transport, each followed by a dozer tender carrying tools and roughly 110 gallons of diesel. "We burn about 80 gallons a day in diesel for each dozer," he added. A smaller, faster Type 2 dozer (Dozer 45)—purchased for the department by the LAFD Foundation—would join later.

On the morning of January 7, Rich was in the North Valley scouting potential quarters for a hand crew we knew we'd need. When the Palisades Fire popped, he pivoted south. The dozers were staged at Fire Station 88 in Sherman Oaks, but he didn't send them into West LA down Sunset Blvd—the obvious route most people would take. "I never go that way," he said. "We offload on Reseda and come up and over the top on Dirt Mulholland, then down. That gives me access to every single ridge on the Santa Monica Mountains. Put the iron on the spine of the range, keep it mobile, and choose terrain that lets you work."

From top access off Michael Lane, Rich tied in with one of his operators, highly competent Heavy Equipment Operator Wes Schroeder. Wes dropped the dozer where it could matter, then scouted ahead in a utility truck—the chase vehicle that ferries fuel, lights, and tools—and reached the point of origin from above before Rich did.

His mission is clear. I asked him to explain the dozer's job without jargon. "The bulldozers are making access to the fire's perimeter," he said. "Their job is to remove all of the burning debris— lumber, weeds, grass—and create a barrier between burned and unburned fuels. The goal is to tie it from ridges down to the backs of houses or to natural barriers—rock outcrops, cliffs, beach, roads." Containment is just that: dirt doesn't burn. A dozer can carve a 16-foot mineral-earth line in minutes that would take a boots-on-the-ground hand crew hours.

But lines are only as good as the ground will allow, and that early terrain was too steep to "wrap" under the edge. Dozers began to bog. "Guys were worried about potentially rolling over," he said. With aircraft prioritized over burning neighborhoods—and winds shredding water drops into mist—Rich shifted gears.

"We started directing our other dozers to a contingency line, the next ridge to the east," he said. "Indirect line on the ridge—push all the brush off it—so the fire runs up to the top where there's no more fuel and goes out, in theory. And if it makes a hard push, air tankers and helicopters can tie it back to that line." That ridge was Farmer's (listed on maps as Rogers Trail), northeast of the initial run between Sullivan Canyon and Mandeville Canyon. The plan was sound. The winds had other ideas.

"We had little vortices—tornado effects—throwing embers in

Erik Scott

all directions," Rich said. "I had to wear a chin strap just to keep my helmet from blowing off… embers hit me in the throat and went down my shirt." Up top, smoke cleared away from the ridge, but the steepness and crosswinds made drops ineffective—water and retardant were blown into neighborhoods. The fire kept spotting, rolling, and building mass down-canyon."

Listening to him describe it brought me right back to what I experienced that night of January 7th at the Will Rogers command post: it felt like a hurricane made of fire. By mid-afternoon on Day One, they pivoted completely to indirect—building the big box—a perimeter designed to contain the fire through indirect means.

He chose West Ridge (labeled "West Mandeville Fire Road" on some maps) as the anchor to keep the fire out of Mandeville Canyon. "I have to make that decision without anybody, because no one else is up there to understand what I'm dealing with," he told me. "Tie it north to south and into the houses. That's why I went to that one—to protect homes."

That first night, they pushed "three blades wide." Day Two, they doubled it. They also opened Sullivan Canyon—daylight only—because of the utility corridors there. "Two 30-inch high-pressure gas mains," he said. "Working at night over all those pipelines could be catastrophic. In daylight, with gas company reps, placards, and eyes on, we tied it in."

Down below, an LA County dozer (Dozer 5) started up from the bottom to meet Rich's lines. Then Rich got the call: "We cannot get apparatus from the east to the west because all of the lanes are blocked with parked cars and no keys in them." I asked if pushing cars with a dozer was even on the typical menu. "It's not something we practice or train. It's a lot of personal property," he said. "But when you have no option, it's the only option… It worked really well."

Calm Amidst Chaos

What happened next became one of the most recognizable images of the fire. Seeing a bulldozer on Sunset Boulevard use its blade to push vehicles off the clogged roadway was striking—so visual it went viral and ended up on T-shirts. But it was the right call. Emergency access had to be opened, and Sunset is a major egress route for the public. It wasn't about spectacle; it was about clearing lifelines and keeping people safe.

Mission critical: open egress routes and let engines reach fires that were actively consuming homes.

Several hours later, the wind aligned in Sullivan Canyon above Camp Josepho—a historic Boy Scouts camp and year-round training ground tucked into dense vegetation in Rustic Canyon, with a single narrow access. Rich knows the camp well from training exercises and relationships with staff. "The winds the night before had snapped trees twenty inches around, twenty feet off the ground," he said. "Healthy trees at the bottom of the drainage—snapped."

He reached the site, checked on life safety (everyone had evacuated), and did what he could with a small backhoe to clear debris. But when the wind laid into the canyon, there was no safe way to execute a defensive burn by himself—no lighting crew, no holding resources, no lookout, and nowhere to go if it blew back. He made the right call and got out.

"At 2:17 p.m. on January 8, it came out of the north end like a freight train," he said. "Everything down there went up at once—propane, cars, buildings." Later, he returned to find every structure burned except a cinder block building at the pool. Its construction—no voids, upwind side—helped it survive without intervention.

When I asked about regret, he didn't dodge it. "I regret that with more people in the right spots, we could've done some good work," he said. "But I'm grateful my decision process puts life over property. There was nothing I could've done by myself to make that

Erik Scott

go away. I'm working through that."

It's hard to look people in the eye after they lose a home. Rich is honest about that. I know the feeling—I had to do the same with countless Palisades residents. And like him, I tried to balance that weight with the clarity of what we did save, and the wins that followed.

By the evening of January 10, the wind turned. "Instead of blowing toward the beach, it's pushing west toward Mandeville," he said. The timing mattered: those ridges had already been opened and widened. "To me, the biggest win was Mandeville," he said. "Being able to save Mandeville Canyon." I couldn't agree more. Air tankers painted the ridges. Helicopters connected drops to dozer work. Firing operations along Dirt Mulholland—the only east-west spine in a sea of north-south ridges—stopped the northward advance. What started as a desperate indirect plan on Day One became the backbone of containment on Days 2 through 4.

On January 13, with more help in place, Rich pushed east of the 405 freeway to rehab and reopen another critical fire road. Within days, a separate eastern fire started, ran up a drainage, and hit that newly improved line—then stopped. Not part of the Palisades incident, but made easier to control because the work was already done. That's the theme of Rich's world: the best heavy-equipment work is invisible, done before the flame front arrives.

Dozer lines can look stark on green hills. Rich doesn't argue that. He just asks the public to weigh the tradeoffs honestly and consider updated practices. "When you remove vegetation, there's dirt left behind," he said. "People call it a scar. We look at it as a containment line." He favors "shaded fuel breaks"—thinning and limbing brush to a lollipop shape, removing receptive fine fuels underneath, and leaving a mosaic that reads more natural than a straight dirt stripe while still slowing fire and giving crews a safer place to work.

And the work doesn't end at containment. "After the fire's out, the amount of work that goes into rehabbing everything we did is insane," he told me. Berms get pulled, drains fixed, brush hand-placed to disguise and stabilize slopes. "A year later, with all the knowledge of where our lines were, I couldn't find them. That's the point." He also notes how previous footprints can help: the Topanga side benefited because a prior burn left younger, less-loaded fuels and slowed spread—a natural, if unplanned, fuel break.

When I asked what stayed with him, the first thing Rich mentioned wasn't machinery. It was people. "I truly appreciate the amount of respect and support from the community," he said. Their support turned our Logistics section—led by Captains Moody, Kitahata, and Ruiz—into a Walmart or an Amazon right down the street from the fire: food, water, sports drinks, ChapStick, eye wash—moving where it was needed, when it was needed.

There's a line heavy-equipment bosses live by: keep going while you have the opportunity. On January 7, when direct attack wasn't possible, Rich kept going—east, west, north—until the ridges made a box we could hold. When the wind shifted on January 10 at 5:23 p.m., that quiet work paid off. And later, when a separate fire pushed up a drainage east of the 405, it hit one of those freshly rehabbed lines and stopped. The hero image is the wind-bucked helicopter drop. The less cinematic truth is a 93,000-pound dozer crawling at eight miles per hour, carving a line you can't see from a living room but that stops a fire at 3:00 a.m.

Rich said it best, in his plain way: "The work I do isn't normally during the fire. It's before the fire hits. That's why we're able to be so successful."

By the time the dozers had carved their lines and the aircraft had painted the ridges, another battle was already underway—

Erik Scott

one far less visible, but just as vital. Even the best lines, shaded breaks, and firing operations depended on a supply chain that never stopped.

Chapter 6

THE LIFELINE OF LOGISTICS

"There is an expected destructive, widespread, and potentially
life-threatening windstorm starting Tuesday morning...
All in fire-prone areas should be ready to evacuate."

~ *National Weather Service*

The public usually sees wildfires in terms of flames and rescues. Helicopters bucking wind shear, dozers crawling across
ridges, crews dragging hose through backyards. But another fight
was unfolding in the background—one that determined whether
those frontline efforts could keep going at all. Feeding thousands,
housing them, repairing equipment, setting up command posts—it
was like building a small city overnight. Without logistics, the fight
would have ended before it began.

Captain II Richard Moody, Logistics Section Chief, was already leaning forward before the first flame. On January 6, the National Weather Service sent out a bulletin unlike anything he had
seen in 25 years on the job—destructive winds with the potential
for loss of life. "We'd never seen a message like that," Moody told
me. "It stopped me in my tracks."

The alert warned of gusts between 80 and 100 miles per hour,
widespread damage, and extreme fire risk across Los Angeles.

Erik Scott

Moody didn't wait. He immediately called General Services to confirm diesel fuel deliveries, proactively checked in with food vendors, and started lining up resources. "Anytime you see 80 to 100 mile-an-hour winds in a forecast, you know what's coming," he said. "That's when I start calling fuel reps, food vendors, making sure we've got contracts lined up. Because within four or five hours of a destructive fire, we're going to need all of it—diesel, sack lunches, trailers, sleeping quarters. You can't wait for the call. You've got to be ahead of it."

On the morning of January 7, Moody was already in West LA at Fire Station 59, supporting a command post for a presidential visit. The city was balancing national security and looming disaster at the same time. "We had Biden in town visiting his granddaughter, and Trump was preparing to come back into office in days," Moody recalled. "Secret Service, LAPD, Fire—everybody was staged at 59's. And then the dispatch hit."

He stepped outside and saw it. A massive column of smoke was rising over the Palisades, straight into a crystal-clear sky. "It looked like a volcano," Moody said. "With those winds, I knew it was going to be destructive." He didn't wait for orders. He left Fire Station 59 immediately, heading for Will Rogers State Beach, where he began laying the foundation for a base camp.

He arrived alone, but not for long. Captain Andrew Ruiz— usually the tip of the spear on fires—was unexpectedly pulled into the world of logistics. "I was at the Training Center when I got the call from Moody," Ruiz told me. "'This is going to be a campaign fire. I'm going to need you and maybe your whole shop.' That was the moment everything shifted."

Ruiz shut down In-Service Training classes on the spot. Forklifts, flatbeds, drivers, electricians—every resource under his command was redirected toward building out the backbone of the fire. "Think of it as building a mobile city out of nothing," he said. "Thousands of firefighters are coming in. They need food, hydration, medical supplies, gear, fuel, a place to shower, and even somewhere to sleep. Without it, the frontline stops."

The frontline was heavily tested. That first night, crews worked 12 to 14 hours with nothing to eat until stacks of donated pizzas showed up at Will Rogers. Ruiz smiled, remembering it: "We pushed that food right to the line. That was survival fuel."

The conditions at base camp were not much better than on the ridge. Inside the command trailers, it felt like an amusement park ride—walls shaking, slide-outs pulled in so they wouldn't blow over. "Honestly," Ruiz admitted, "I thought one of the command trailers might tip." Outside, embers set grass alight inside the perimeter, and firefighters stomped out flames with their boots. LAPD officers, unused to fire behavior, expressed their lack of comfort. "We're used to it," Ruiz said. "But they weren't. It rattled them."

Even the communications lifeline was severely strained. Cell towers were down. Radios cut in and out. Orders had difficulty reaching the field. The difference came in the form of donated Starlinks—hand-delivered, jury-rigged with adapters and generators, even bolted to bulldozers. "Without that, we were done," Moody said flatly. "Once we plugged in, we had email, phones, and data again. That's what kept logistics alive."

If Moody and Ruiz built the framework, Captain Thomas Kitahata lived the fire from both sides of the line. Stationed at Fire Station 69 in the Palisades, he was a respected officer and deeply embedded in the community long before the flames came. He and I had even shared a lighter moment on Netflix's Bake Squad (Season 2, Episode 8, "Bring on the Heat"), standing side by side in front of cameras for something sweet instead of scorching.

On January 7, Kitahata rushed from his home in Thousand

Oaks, grabbed his gear, and tried to tie in with engine companies already in the Highlands. Smoke, embers, and gridlocked traffic made it nearly impossible. "It was like nothing I'd ever seen before," he told me. "Never in a million years would I have expected this to happen here."

Redirected into logistics, Kitahata became Base Camp Manager at Will Rogers, working under Moody and with Ruiz. His shorthand description: "Everything from bathrooms to batteries." For 30 straight days, he kept the lifeline flowing—food, restrooms, power, and equipment for thousands of firefighters, before taking a day off.

His perspective carried the weight of decades. In thirty-seven years on the job, he had been deployed to 9/11, Hurricane Katrina, the 1994 Northridge earthquake, and the 1992 riots. He knew what chaos looked like, and the Palisades ranked right alongside those disasters. But this one was personal—because Fire Station 69 sat in the middle of it.

The Palisades community had always embraced Station 69. Years earlier, when city orders forced the crew to shut off water sprinklers, neighbors stepped in to fund and build a landscaping project that transformed the station grounds. Kitahata shared a photo of the plaque commemorating that 2018 beautification effort—a small but telling symbol of the bond between firefighters and residents.

That bond was tested in the fire. Months later, some residents shouted at crews when working out on the beach, convinced they had saved the firehouse while homes burned. Kitahata patiently explained: the station had been defended by off-duty firefighters who came in voluntarily, not by members abandoning neighborhoods. And as for the fire trucks parked at the beach? Those were ladder trucks without hose or water, strategically staged by logistics while their crews were reassigned to engines that could fight fire. "People didn't know," Kitahata told me. "And that's why communication matters."

He also reminded me of the scale of the challenge: only 12 firefighters at Station 69, and 6 more at Station 23, against hundreds of homes burning simultaneously. "That's all we had at first," he said. "12 and 6. Think about that."

In the days that followed, Kitahata fielded calls directly from community members who had his personal number. He escorted families back into the burn zone. One couple sifted through ash until they found the engagement ring they had bought decades earlier, long since replaced but priceless in memory. Another family wept as they realized the magnitude of what had been lost, with Kitahata standing quietly beside them. "After a while," he admitted, "I stopped going all the way in with them. It was too much."

There were also moments of grace. Tom and Rita Hanks, who had a family home in the Palisades, called Kitahata and later sent an In-N-Out truck to the base camp that fed thousands of firefighters. They asked for no fanfare—just a small handwritten sign in a window: Thank you, firefighters. —Tom & Rita.

Sue Kohl, a community leader who lost her own home (more about her story later), came by Station 69 weekly with baked goods. "She had nothing left, but she kept showing up with cookies," Kitahata said, shaking his head in quiet admiration.

Through it all, the firehouse doors remained open, literally and figuratively. Neighbors dropped by for coffee, just as they always had. Even in rubble, the station remained a gathering place.

Kitahata's reflection mirrored what Ruiz and Moody had also told me: logistics may not make headlines, but it was the lifeline of the incident. It kept the fight going. It gave the community a tether to their firefighters. And it offered, in the smallest gestures—pizza boxes, sack lunches, coffee shared across a table—a reminder that survival is a collective act.

Kitahata reminded me that logistics was never a one-department show. "We worked hand in hand with everybody—DOT, DWP, LAPD, General Services, SoCal Gas, Street Services, CHP, even the National Guard," he said. "I relied heavily on my buddies in those departments. We also used food trucks and community members to help feed thousands of first responders and critical workers. It was very similar to the large-scale operations we dealt with during the pandemic. We're only able to do what we do because of that partnership. Like they say—it takes a village."

"I've been to a lot of disasters," Kitahata said finally. "This one changed me. It made me appreciate my fellow firefighters even more. And it made me believe in the resilience of this community. They're rebuilding already. They're not leaving. And that gives me hope."

The lifeline of logistics never made the evening news, but it kept the fireground moving. Every sandwich bag, every refueled rig, every Starlink bolted to a bulldozer meant the frontline could push a little farther. Moody, Ruiz, and Kitahata proved that survival in the Palisades wasn't only about the flames—it was about the systems and people who quietly sustained the fight.

As the last families escaped the canyons and the fire's perimeter began to hold, another battle was already underway — against exhaustion, misinformation, and the weight that comes after surviving the unthinkable.

Chapter 7

THE WEIGHT OF THE FLAMES

*"In a crisis, rumor always outruns fact unless someone
is pushing the truth just as hard."*

~ *Erik Scott*

By the morning after Day One, the Palisades Fire had already made history. Nearly 20,000 acres had burned, thousands of residents were displaced, but we didn't yet fully grasp the magnitude of destruction—that entire neighborhoods had already been reduced to ash. There was no time for reflection. The fire was still moving, and so were we.

On the line, the sprint shifted into a marathon. Crews who had worked 36 hours straight finally rotated out as fresh strike teams arrived from across California. Dozers cut new lines along ridges, hand crews cleared brush, and engines carried out tactical patrols in neighborhoods where embers still smoldered under decks, fences, and rooflines. Saving homes wasn't only about stopping the fire front—it was about constant vigilance afterward.

The smoke was its own enemy. It wasn't just chaparral—it was homes, cars, plastics, and batteries burning together. The air was a cocktail of toxins; a hazard we knew might take a toll long after the flames were out. Firefighters worked in masks when possible, but many pressed on without, eyes and lungs stinging with every breath. Still, they pushed forward, defending one street at a time.

For the public, information became a lifeline. Early on, we told residents exactly where they could go if they had to leave in a hurry, such as Westwood Recreation Center, which we made sure to note was pet-friendly. For many, leaving without their animals wasn't an option, and that detail mattered.

For me, the job was to give the public steady information. Dozens of news outlets crowded Will Rogers State Beach. Residents wanted answers. National networks wanted context. International outlets wanted perspective. By now, it wasn't just national news—it was world news. When the sun set here, it was rising across the globe, and they wanted updates.

We built out a robust media branch. Before every update, we checked with Operations, LAPD, and the Evacuation Branch. People needed to know which roads were open, where buses were staged, and when they could expect updates. Reporters were a helpful force multiplier. When we gave them facts, they carried those facts to millions.

Misinformation was a constant battle. At one point, rumors online claimed that critical facilities were being evacuated when they weren't. We verified with field crews and corrected it publicly before it spread further—because in a fire like this, bad information spreads as fast as embers. That became the rhythm: verify, update, push it out fast.

And that was where the weight really landed: not just in fighting fire, but in striving to be the voice people trusted.

~~~~~

By nightfall of Day Two, exhaustion weighed on everyone. Firefighters slept in engines. Command staff nodded off between calls. Families lingered in shelters with only what they carried out. Yet despite the toll, resilience showed—neighbors helping neighbors, crews rotating and returning, a city refusing to break.

Somewhere in those long hours, it hit me that this wasn't just another wildfire. Its size, speed, and ferocity were unlike anything Los Angeles had faced. For the men and women on the line, this fire would define careers. For me, it became clear my responsibility wasn't just to describe the fire. It was for us to give the city a steady voice in chaos.

Even as the fire pressed on, the message stayed steady—anchored in the same guidance Brian Humphrey taught me and that I'd relied on since the first hours of the incident: tell people what is happening, what we're doing about it, and what it means to them. It wasn't a new idea, but it remained the compass for how we communicated under pressure.

~~~~~

The Palisades Fire had already shown its fury. But in the middle of destruction, there were also clear successes—moments where preparation, quick action, and determination made the difference.

On the fire's worst days, entire neighborhoods survived because firefighters stood their ground. Engines backed into driveways, hose stretched across patios, and tactical patrols snuffed embers one by one. In Marquez Knolls, strike teams held cul-de-sacs even as flames pushed through the hillsides. Crews refused to leave, then immediately went back to extinguish spot fires. Those decisions meant dozens of homes remained standing when the smoke cleared.

Erik Scott

Some areas weren't as fortunate. The ABC streets in Pacific Palisades were reduced to rubble—only foundations and chimneys remained. Walking those streets was sobering. Families returned to find everything gone, while just across the way, some homes still stood.

Communicating that reality to the public was one of the hardest tasks: balancing the grief of those who lost everything with recognition of the efforts that had saved other neighborhoods. It was a reminder that success and tragedy often stood side by side, separated by only a few feet of ground and a shift in the wind.

When hydrants were inaccessible or pressure dropped, firefighters improvised. Engines drafted water from backyard pools, and portable pumps were placed into reservoirs. In one section of the Highlands, companies built a relay system, leapfrogging water engine to engine, to keep hose streams alive. These weren't textbook solutions—they were practical fixes that bought time and kept embers from taking more homes.

By the end of those operational periods, the acres lost were enormous, and the destruction was sobering. Wind-driven fires have produced some of the deadliest outcomes in recent U.S. history—tragically, 102 lives were lost in the 2023 Lahaina Fire and 85 in the 2018 Camp Fire—stark reminders of just how fast these events turn deadly. Yet alongside the devastation were undeniable wins: neighborhoods intact, thousands of lives protected, and a city that continued to function under extraordinary pressure.

The lesson was clear: success wasn't measured only in updating acreage and containment numbers. It was measured in the relentless firefight, the families who evacuated safely, and the resilience that kept Los Angeles moving forward.

Chapter 8

THE CALM VOICE

"Credibility became our currency. It bought us trust.
When people believed us, they acted.
And when they acted, lives were saved."

~ *Erik Scott*

By Day Three, the fire's pace had slowed, but the demand for information had not. Evacuation updates, road closures, damage assessments, and health warnings had to be pushed out constantly and without confusion.

At the Incident Command Post on Will Rogers State Beach, the pace never stopped. The trailers rattled in the wind, radios hissed without pause, and rows of laptops glowed in smoke-tinged air. Inside, about a hundred public information officers rotated through shifts. Some drafted press releases, others updated progression maps, still others staffed call centers—answering desperate residents in English, Spanish, and beyond. Translators hammered out evacuation orders in real time. Their grind wasn't visible to the public, but without them, order would have fractured.

To keep coverage continuous across a sprawling, multi-incident footprint, we split PIO operations in two. On the south side at Will Rogers (where I led the Media Division), Jake Heflin orchestrated daily coordination and battle rhythm. On the north side at Zuma Beach, Ken Haskett worked alongside CAL FIRE's Thomas Shoots and his team to synchronize messaging, maps, and field intel. That structure—one voice, two hubs—made the difference between noise and clarity.

This was the lifeline.

~~~~~

In the middle of those long, back-to-back operational days, surrounded by radios, cameras, and the constant churn of information, I was reminded that calm doesn't just steady those already in command—it teaches those still learning what leadership sounds like. Among the many people who rotated through the Public Information Office during the Palisades Fire was a young intern and cadet named Henry Berkson. He represented the next generation of the department: curious, eager, and unshakably optimistic.

When I first met Henry Berkson, he wasn't yet an LAFD cadet or intern—just a teenager standing near the Los Angeles River on a day the entire city seemed to be watching. Helicopters hovered overhead during a swift-water rescue that was live on every news channel. After the incident, Henry approached and asked, "Hey, are you Captain Scott?" When I said yes, he grinned and said, "I'm your biggest fan. I've watched you on YouTube for years as the department spokesperson."

It was 2021, near the tail end of the pandemic, and his enthusiasm stood out immediately. Not long after, I helped bring him on as an intern at our Community Liaison Office downtown. "That was actually through you, Captain Scott, when we met at that river rescue and then that opened up an opportunity for me to come in and work as an intern with you and the rest of the team at the Community Liaison Office," he later recalled.

From there, we assisted Henry in joining Cadet Post 81 in the San Fernando Valley. "I gained lots of good skills there relating directly to the fire service, as well as really good skills through the internship at City Hall East—in both digital media and communications—and typical office skills that can help anyone in any field." Within a year, he was certified to ride along on engines and trucks. "I started riding out at 27s, then at 78, and I've gotten certified to ride along on a truck so I can go on light forces and task forces, as well as on rescues. I just recently got my EMT."

Before the Palisades Fire, my team and I had discussed that if a major wind-driven fire broke within city limits, someone from headquarters would need to bring our full communications set-up—battery packs, lights, cameras, chargers, tripods, even an EZ-Up—to support Public Information operations before a formal Incident Command Post could stand up. Henry remembered that conversation when the fire erupted.

"I was at school," he said. "I ran down to my car and got my radio and started listening to the command channel. I heard conditions deteriorating. I heard exactly what you heard when you were there." He texted to check in, eager to assist, but with traffic gridlocked and bulldozers clearing cars from Sunset Boulevard, we agreed it was safer for him to wait.

By the third day, when operations stabilized, Henry arrived at headquarters. Those were intense hours of nonstop interviews and community updates as questions poured in about cause, evacuations, and water supply. "That night we went out to the ICP at Zuma Beach, and that was like being introduced to a whole different world," he said. "I'd never been on an incident that large. I wasn't used to seeing the entire ICS system really put into play, and it was fascinating."

Erik Scott

Zuma Beach looked like a city built overnight—rows of strike teams, communications trailers, kitchen units, and supply trucks—and the same was true for the southern ICP at Will Rogers, which was kept running by Captains Kitahata, Moody, and Ruiz. "There were trailers from one end of the parking lot to the other," Henry said. "Engines, strike teams, the physical command posts, the kitchen unit—all these different things I'd never seen before."

We laughed, remembering the cameras. "I recall that first day we had a documentary crew with us. It was pretty interesting to be followed around by cameras—welcome to your world, I guess." Then his tone shifted. "The National Guard being there as well—it wasn't a war, but it made it feel like one. A war against the fire. The military was standing up outside of this fire with rifles on them, and it was not something I was used to seeing."

Henry stayed six days. "The main thing that stood out to me was your consistency—just the fact that you were returning there every single day to the ICP or around the fire perimeter to constantly give new information. That consistency—it showed me what leadership looks like when everything's burning."

He also remembered a photograph that stayed with him. "Once repopulation began, there was that photo of you with some homeowners along PCH, helping them repopulate, seeing that their home was destroyed and being a person there for them in that time of heartbreak."

Those homeowners—an elderly couple whose house had burned to its foundation—later sent me a heartfelt email of thanks. Their words still remind me that compassion carries as much weight as command. Their story, and that photograph, would stay with me long after the fire; I return to it later in this book, in the chapter on recovery, because what happened that day captured the quiet side of resilience that statistics can never show.

When Henry returned to school, normal life felt hollow. "Going back to school after that was rough," he said. "It felt like I was a part of something very, very moving—more than just being a cadet. Having it end abruptly and just going back to school—it didn't make me the happiest." I told him that was understandable; after living inside something so intense, ordinary life takes time to feel normal again.

He laughed when he called himself "a radio nerd." After long days helping with media coordination, he volunteered at night with the Communications Unit, monitoring channels and learning dispatch procedures. That kind of curiosity and ambition, combined with humility, defines what's best about our cadets.

He finished quietly. "Some of my friends lost homes. One of my parents' close friends, unfortunately, their house got destroyed. Some cadets as well—some had damaged homes, some lost their homes. For me personally, I'm just happy that I could provide some form of support with my abilities. I'm glad that I was able to be a part of such a wide range of support staff to help with that incident."

Our cadets remind us that the future of the fire service is bright. They arrive eager, self-driven, and humble. They study radio traffic, learn the craft from the ground up, and carry a quiet determination to help others. Watching Henry grow through those six days—and in the years since—reminded me that leadership is a circle: you light the path for someone, and someday they'll do the same for someone else.

Working alongside Henry was a reminder of how wide the circle of service truly extends—seasoned officers, civilian specialists, cadets, interns, and volunteers all pulling in the same direction. The Palisades Fire had grown beyond any one division or discipline; it required unity of message and purpose. By the time

Erik Scott

Henry packed up his gear and returned to school, our Public Information operation was hitting its stride—two hubs working in lockstep, information moving as fast as the fire itself, and every update shaped with the same steady, deliberate communication we'd practiced since hour one.

~~~~~

The stakes were clear from the very first hours. We issued evacuation orders for high-threat zones and urged people to leave immediately. Not long after, the fast-moving fire reached those areas. Early evacuation made escape routes safe and more accessible.

Later, when we told residents on a wind-exposed ridge to go, they listened. Flames overtook that very ridge soon after. And when we pushed "leave now" for the Highlands, thousands moved out before roads clogged. Those weren't just words—they were survival.

I carried those images with me: headlights streaming down canyon roads, buses transporting seniors to safety, strike teams shielding the last of the evacuees. Every clear sentence was a lifeline. Every minute mattered.

~~~~~

Jake Heflin, like most Public Information Officers, did not plan on becoming one. That resonated with me because when I joined the fire department, I didn't know the position even existed. Yet both of us eventually found our way to it—the intersection of service, communication, and calm under pressure—first drawn by necessity, and then purpose.

"I am currently a Long Beach Fire Department Battalion Chief assigned to Operations," Heflin said. "But at the time of the Palisades incident, I was a Fire Captain assigned to our Community Services Division and also had collateral duties as a Public Information Officer, and was requested and assigned to the Palisades incident public information shop under the CAL FIRE incident management team."

Heflin's fire service journey began in 1991 with the Orange County Fire Authority, serving the communities of Emerald Bay and Irvine. After completing paramedic school at Saddleback College, he worked as a field supervisor for American Medical Response (AMR) before earning what he called his "lottery win"— a position with the Long Beach Fire Department. Over the years, he moved from operations to community services, where an unexpected opportunity to work with Community Emergency Response Team (CERT) volunteers introduced him to public information.

"I had no thought about pursuing anything related to public information ever," he admitted. "I never really knew that much about the position... but I found fulfillment in communicating with the public and developing relationships with the community." That same realization would shape both of our careers.

Three or four days into the Palisades response, Jake's assignment cleared, and he joined our expanding public information team. The moment he stepped into the operations briefing at Zuma Beach, the gravity of the situation hit him. "The size and scope... was significant," he told me. "You realize this is a big, big deal." Soon after, he was transferred to the Southern Unified Command Post at Will Rogers State Beach, where he and I worked side by side organizing one of the most complex media operations of our careers.

Trust was instantaneous because it had already been built through countless fires. Jake and I had responded to major incidents

Erik Scott

across Los Angeles and deployed together to wildfires throughout the state. We'd been tested under pressure—on the line, in the smoke, in moments that left no room for hesitation or ego. Those experiences forge something deeper than friendship: a bond tempered by long nights, hard calls, and the unspoken understanding that when things go bad, you can count on the other person to be there.

The same was true with LA County's Ken Haskett, another seasoned veteran I've had the privilege of working beside on multiple large-scale incidents. His calm, deliberate leadership has always commanded respect. Jake had served with Ken on the 2020 August Complex Fire—one of the largest wildfires in California's history—and that shared history among the three of us proved invaluable when seconds mattered and clarity counted.

In this job, there are many firefighters—especially seasoned officers—you forge steel-like bonds with. Shared emergencies have a way of burning away pretense and revealing who people truly are. I've been blessed to serve beside countless men and women I'd trust with my life—people who would drop everything if one of their own needed help. That's the brotherhood.

Jake Heflin leads with calm under pressure, compassion, and precision. Those are the qualities that set him apart when it matters most. He's the kind of person you could hand your family's safety to and know every detail would be handled with care, competence, and heart. He doesn't just manage chaos—he steadies everyone around him while doing it.

A citizen of both the Osage and Cherokee Nations, he's been a strong voice for emergency preparedness in tribal communities, teaching courses and helping develop tribal CERT programs. "To serve my people in that way," he said, "has been a passion of mine."

So when he arrived at Will Rogers, I didn't have to give a long briefing or a checklist. The first thing I told him was simple: "Jake, do your thing."

He did.

"My whole goal was to take the pressure off of your team," he said. "You focus on the requirements being put on you from your leadership, and I will handle the rest."

And he meant it. Within hours, Jake established a system to process the flood of inquiries coming from every direction—local, national, and international media all desperate for accurate information. "We were dealing with an international media storm," he recalled. "There were issues about media credentials, reporter's access, endless interviews, and fire cause speculation. We had to intake every request, assign a PIO, and make sure that loop was closed."

What made Jake's leadership unique was his inclusion of civilian staff. Long Beach sent three communications professionals, including Melanie Miller, who built the media-tracking system that became our lifeline. "That tracking system was the win," Jake said. "We never had that kind of demand before."

I viewed Melanie, Johnathan Garcia, Laath Martin, and the rest of the civilian team as absolute rock stars. They showed up with outstanding attitudes and an even better work ethic—no drama, no ego, just relentless focus and teamwork. Their professionalism elevated the entire operation. Because of their system, I was able to manage in-depth interviews with outlets like *The Wall Street Journal* and CNN while still ensuring that smaller, community-based, or international crews were treated with the same level of attention and respect.

Heflin's philosophy about communications mirrored my own. "Operations drives everything that we do in the fire service," he said. "However, the community wants to know... and there's this instantaneous desire for information that really requires a diligent effort... Our goal is to stay out in front in messaging and not let the messaging run the incident."

He also understood that the messenger mattered as much as the message. "That helps bring that sense of calmness," he said. "And that is a critical part."

I often can be heard sharing this quote:

"In an emergency, you must treat information as a commodity as important as food, water, and shelter."

The Palisades Fire proved it. Information—timely, accurate, consistent—wasn't an accessory. It was survival. Deliver those three, and you earn the fourth: credibility. And credibility matters, because when you're giving true EPI (Emergency Public Information) and guiding evacuations, people must believe every word.

When I asked Jake how the Palisades Fire affected him personally, his answer reached back decades. In 1993, as a young firefighter in Laguna Beach, Jake lived through the Laguna Firestorm that destroyed his neighborhood. "It came within fifteen feet of my home," he remembered. "Driving through the Palisades, it was a flashback. I could empathize with the people experiencing catastrophic loss."

That empathy drove his commitment to sharing stories of resilience—like the heroic rescue by Los Angeles County Fire Captain Malcolm Dicks, who pulled a woman from a burning vehicle trapped on a rock. "That's the true story," Jake said. "People helping people. Disasters are the great equalizer."

He paused, then added, "To be a part of that—even in a small way—was an honor."

And it was. For both of us.

~~~~~

The challenge wasn't only putting out information—it was outpacing rumor.

Scanner chatter spread half-truths online within minutes. A false report claimed a major coastal highway was open. It wasn't. Another said regional hospitals were evacuating. They weren't. Left unchecked, either could have created panic.

Our job was to correct the record before chaos spread. "Turn left, not right. This zone is mandatory, not voluntary. Do not return yet." Words sharpened into direction; direction sharpened into action. And as the fire transitioned into recovery, that same clarity mattered just as much—especially when warning residents about hazardous materials, toxic ash, and the protocols for safe fire-debris removal on burned-out properties. Information protected people during the fire, and it protected them afterward.

Nick Schuler, CAL FIRE's Deputy Director of Communications, had spent nearly three decades balancing firelines and headlines. He saw the same dynamic on the CAL FIRE side. "The sheer amount of misinformation—both intentional and unintentional—was profound," he said. "In many cases, it forced us to pull public information officers away from critical duties just to address false allegations."

That constant tug-of-war made it clear: facts couldn't simply be accurate—they had to be fast, consistent, and repeated until they stuck.

~~~~~

Another key component of the LAFD's communications is the LAFD's Public Service Officer (PSO) who plays a vital behind-the-scenes role in keeping both the public and the media informed during emergencies and major incidents.

Erik Scott

By design, the PSO desk runs 24/7, a one-person office seated on the edge of our 911 dispatch floor. Margaret Stewart has held that seat for over a decade— part of nearly 20 years on the department—after seven years of active-duty military service, six in the corporate world (where she earned an MBA), and a long run as a Search & Rescue canine handler (Bo for live-find; Rose and Veya for human-remains detection). That breadth of experience shows up in how she frames the mission: disciplined, structured, unflappable.

She calls the workspace "the cave." There are no exterior windows, lights kept low to reduce eye strain. Six televisions stay locked on the local news stations; multiple radio speakers carry three dispatch channels plus the fireground tacs; five stacked monitors surface the CAD (Computer Aided Dispatch) feed, while large wall screens push situational data to anyone who steps in. A single interior door opens to the 911 floor; you can literally hear a call-taker shout "structure" through the wall while the incident materializes on a CAD line. It's downtown, a few blocks from City Hall and tight to the 101—close enough that news and command are never far away.

Scale matters. In Los Angeles, we handle roughly 1,500 emergency incidents per day. Only a handful meet the threshold for a citywide alert, but the tempo swings.

"There are days I don't send any, and days I send a dozen," she said. The PSO runs LAFD Alerts (public opt-in) for incidents of significance and uses Everbridge as the engine behind those alerts. The same platform can deliver internal, staff-only notifications when we need to inform the department without triggering public messaging.

Stewart writes alerts the same way every time—on purpose. Consistency reduces friction for readers and for the PSO under stress. With address and resource fields now auto-populated, her work is the narrative: clear, structured, time-stamped entries that grow into a reliable thread. "If it's written the same way, I'm faster—and it's easier to process on the other end."

In the opening stretch of the Palisades Fire, that discipline met rapidly evolving conditions. The initial evacuation workflow relied on ArcGIS polygons—drawing street-based boundaries as the situation changed by the minute. Stewart worked shoulder-to-shoulder with partners from the Emergency Management Department (EMD—notably Jennifer Lazo—and on the phone with Rene Gonzalez (our GIS chief) to craft boundaries that matched WEA (Wireless Emergency Alerts) messaging and embedded maps on LAFD. org. Meanwhile, Captain Gayle Sonoda slid into the PSO office to help, and the phone lines never stopped.

Two weeks in, the city began transitioning to Genasys, a new mapping/alerting backbone that changed the mechanics of how evacuations were defined and published. That cut friction, but not the pressure. "You can't gather information and disseminate information at the same time," she said. When the radios are busy, field PIOs aren't yet on scene, and the media line won't stop ringing, something has to give. For the first time in her tenure, she shut the phones off in short intervals—not to avoid the public, but so she could collect enough verified information to alert the public accurately.

The Palisades Fire didn't arrive alone. "Over those first three days, we had six major emergency brush fires with evacuations," Stewart said. "People forget it wasn't just the Palisades."

One of those was the Sunset Fire in the Runyon Canyon area, which ignited on January 8 in the Hollywood Hills, after the Palisades Fire was already fully engaged. Although it shared the same name as the January 7 Sunset Fire, this was a separate incident. Aircraft were redirected at once; had that window closed, a large swath of Hollywood could have been lost. Stewart did something atypical for us: she called the news desks directly—"put me on now"—to push a live, immediate evacuation message while the orders were formalized. That's what the job requires: measured urgency, without guesswork.

The physical toll was blunt. "I didn't leave the building for 28 days," she said. "At one point, it was three days before I got any sleep." It became a mantra born of necessity: "I just live here now."

Tea appeared at her elbow. Someone heated a shoulder pack. Colleagues learned the rhythms of the cave. The calls ran the spectrum—earnest questions from residents without internet access; media hungry for verified updates; and, amid heightened public emotion, a share of screaming, venting, and blame that landed on the only number people could find.

And then there was the "talking injury." After two relentless weeks and "a couple hundred at least" interviews across TV, radio, and international outlets, she realized her tongue was rubbed raw—a strange byproduct of long-healed jaw trauma and nonstop speech. "I couldn't eat or drink for a while," she said. Occupational hazards, PSO edition.

Beyond alerts and interviews, Stewart's remit includes the three primary social platforms (Facebook, Instagram, X), the rolling, time-stamped incident pages on LAFD.org, and our Flickr archive, which functions as the closest thing the department has to a photo library. It's administrative, operational, and public-facing all at once—with a risk surface to match.

"Say one thing wrong and the entire department—even the city—could suffer," she said. "You're always on the record. What you say can be on the front page of the *LA Times*."

She is careful even with back-channel vocal tics on calls—an "mm-hmm" can be misheard as agreement and laundered into attribution.

The PSO maintains two lines: the main media/public line and an internal LAFD-only line that always takes priority. More than once, she ended a live interview to pick up the internal ring, knowing it might carry the update the city needed to hear next. That is the governing ethic: accuracy first, velocity a close second, and reputation protected by both.

When asked what stands out most, Stewart talks about shared endurance and support among the Metro Fire Communication Chiefs, EMD partners, and the PSO bench that grew as relief arrived. An operational cadence was forged under pressure including a refined alert-mapping system so the team could execute quickly. Those kinds of process improvements are a quiet kind of win.

Her closing perspective should land with anyone who lived through January: "Every firefighter wearing a badge—every officer—was doing everything they possibly could. We met circumstances beyond our control. There were countless individual acts of bravery and dedication that will never make a headline, but they were there—every day."

That's the PSO in one line: closest to the noise, closest to the facts, and trusted to tell the story right.

~~~~~

The National Weather Service had warned that a severe wind event was likely. That's why—in the days and hours leading up to January 7—I beat the drum so hard with reporters about readiness: prep your go-kits, know your routes, expect rapid changes, and evacuate early. We also pre-deployed resources citywide in key wildland-urban interface areas and augmented our dispatch and Air Ops posture, positioning for a fast hit the moment a start occurred. I said it repeatedly on the news because it mattered: early beats perfect.

Mid-deployment, The Wall Street Journal reached out. They didn't want a post-mortem; they wanted clarity while the fight was still on. I didn't hesitate to give them the interview because clarity saves lives.

Logistics built me a "studio" from scratch. They rolled a metal Conex box into position, bolted steps to the side, ran a generator for power, and hung a wall-sized progression map that our GIS team printed an hour earlier. Starlink dishes brought bandwidth where there was none. Outside, radios hissed, and the wind bullied the trailers. Inside that steel box, the assignment was simple: explain chaos in plain English.

We started with the fundamentals that the public could use. In extreme wind, the gap between a quick knockdown and a weeks-long disaster is measured in minutes, not hours. That's why we had leaned forward on readiness, pre-placement, and messaging. When the first new start hit, resources and aircraft moved quickly; when the next one ignited, those units pivoted. Emergency alerts went out within minutes to buy time on narrow canyon roads.

I laid out what a single live shot can't show: embers traveling far ahead of the main front; hose streams bending in wind; hydrants at elevation struggling as tanks worked to keep up with demand; engines drafting from swimming pools and setting up water shuttles; tactical patrols leapfrogging through neighborhoods to stamp out spot fires before they became block-wide losses. Aircraft bought us time during the day, but that first night, with winds shredding drops mid-air and safety margins eroding, we stood them down and resumed at first light when conditions allowed.

I tried to translate fire behavior without jargon: topography-driven fires follow ridges and drainages; wind-driven fires behave like a freight train—they go where the wind goes. Under those conditions, you don't "stop" a head fire in the open. You buy time: structure defense, evacuations before traffic seizes, and cut line where it can hold.

We also addressed the multi-incident reality. By the following day, multiple named fires were pulling resources across steep, road-poor terrain. Command integrated with CAL FIRE Incident Management Team and split the Public Information enterprise north/south—Ken Haskett with Thomas Shoots at Zuma, Jake Heflin, and me at Will Rogers—while roughly 100 public information officers cycled through releases, maps, hotlines, and translations so the city heard one clear voice.

When the *Wall Street Journal* aired its interview with me, "Fire Captain Breaks Down Los Angeles Wildfire Disaster | WSJ Hindsight," it reached millions. By then, the immediate evacuations had passed, but the need for clarity hadn't. That interview gave us something different: a chance to explain the scale, the conditions, and the fight in a way the world could finally understand.

In a storm like this, calm isn't a personality trait—it's a tactic.

That makeshift studio was one thread in a much larger web. Logistics was doing a thousand other things: moving fuel and food, clearing choke points, staging equipment, building workspace, delivering parts, and solving the unsolvable so operations could keep fighting. The quiet brilliance of our logistics leaders—officers whose résumés read like a department hall of fame—meant that when something seemed impossible, it still got done.

~~~~~

Leadership during the Palisades Fire wasn't about control—it was about trust. Trusting firefighters to improvise when unexpected conditions arose. Trusting pilots to pause when the air wouldn't let them work, then surge when it did. Trusting PIOs to face cameras, hammer keyboards, and cut through the fog of rumor. It wasn't about pretending everything was under control. It was about steadying the ship—acknowledging the challenges, setting the example, and refusing to let panic seep in.

Schuler agreed that trust was the currency that kept the response from fracturing. "CAL FIRE's work to modernize our website, strengthen our social media presence, and build a robust Public Information Program years before this event proved invaluable during the Palisades and Eaton Fires," he said. "Just as important was the strong, pre-established trust we had with LAFD and LA County Fire—those relationships were critical."

These aren't abstract ideas. They're principles I have taught for years in courses like S-203 and FEMA's L-952—and they were lived, minute by minute, message by message, through smoke, exhaustion, and relentless pressure.

The Palisades Fire reinforced timeless truths: preparation saves lives, but adaptability carries the day. Information is a life-safety commodity—as vital as water or food. Credibility is a powerful leadership tool. And that credibility carried forward. Later, when we found ourselves on red carpets—or even at the Oscars—people paid attention. Not because of tuxedos or spotlights, but because credibility earned in the flames follows you wherever you go.

Chapter 9

OFF-DUTY COURAGE

**"Courage doesn't always look like a full task force on scene—
sometimes it's a single firefighter making
a stand on their own block."**

~ *Erik Scott*

The January 2025 fires were still in full force when another front ignited in Altadena. The Eaton Fire occurred within the Los Angeles County Fire Department's jurisdiction, starting on January 7, 2025, at 6:18 p.m. near Altadena Drive and Midwick Drive. By the time it was contained, the fire had burned 14,021 acres, destroyed 9,414 structures (residential, commercial, and other buildings), and resulted in nineteen confirmed civilian fatalities and nine confirmed firefighter injuries. It started at a moment when resources across Southern California were already stretched thin.

For Los Angeles Fire Department (LAFD) Captain Daniel Lievense and Engineer Matthew Lievense, this wasn't an assignment. It was home. Daniel had spent fifty years in Altadena. He lived next door to his mother. His brother Matthew lived close by. Their childhood street—where they had grown up together and built families of their own—was now directly in the path of a fast-moving firestorm.

On the night the fire started, Daniel was already on duty at a different brush fire. His son, James, called him to report a glow in the hills a couple of miles from their house. Daniel told him to keep an eye on it.

Hours later, around four in the morning, James called again. Smoke was pushing into the neighborhood. One home was already burning. Daniel knew it was time to leave. "Get Mom, get your younger brother, get Grandma, get the pets. You need to evacuate," he told his son.

After hanging up with James, Daniel called his brother, Matthew. He knew what was coming next and needed Matthew moving toward the house. "Just stay with me," Daniel told him over the phone. "Just do this." Matthew, off duty and safe at home in San Dimas, didn't hesitate. He headed straight toward the fire.

When he arrived in Altadena, he described what he saw in stark terms: "It looked like the world was on fire." Houses across the street were burning. Embers were blowing sideways. Heat was radiating off the roadway. "This is your street, Mom. We're gonna save it," he told her in a video.

James, 20 years old, had grown up around the fire service, but this was different. He had never trained for a wildfire, never worked a hose line in real conditions, and never been asked to defend his own home. "He's never been trained for anything like this," Matthew said. "He just has a dad and an uncle who do this. That's it."

Together, James and Matthew went to a nearby Los Angeles County fire station and collected retired hoses, nozzles, and gated wyes—the only equipment available to them. Around 6:15 a.m., Daniel was released from his assignment and drove straight home. The three of them met on the block as daylight pushed faintly through the smoke.

They found a single 2½-inch hydrant they could use. They

stretched roughly 350 feet of hose across several long driveways and created a water curtain between houses to slow the flames. They knocked down spot fires on neighbors' roofs, dragged burning debris away from foundations, sprayed down exposures, kicked away embers, and moved constantly from one burning edge to the next. They weren't simply defending a structure—they were trying to stop the entire block from being overrun.

A Pasadena Fire Department engine arrived, and the crews quickly coordinated on how to divide the work. After a brief discussion, they agreed that the Pasadena crew would defend one side of the block while the Lievense family covered the other. The partnership allowed both sides of the street to be protected during a critical window of time. Eventually, Pasadena advised that they needed to redeploy to another area as the broader incident expanded, and the Lievense family stayed in place, holding their ground, undeterred, and protected their side of the block.

As the fire intensified, transformers blew. High-voltage lines came down. The wind-driven heat was stronger than anything Daniel had ever faced without proper gear. "Never in my life have I experienced going into a fire without the proper equipment," he said later. "It became a little overwhelming. Still brings a little bit of tears to my eyes, like what we did."

They dug-in and fought until the firefront passed.

On Daniel and Matthew's street, twenty homes once stood. Sixteen were ultimately reduced to foundations, but four on that block were still standing when the smoke cleared. On the next street over, they helped save approximately ten additional homes and several apartment buildings from burning. In total, their off-duty stand contributed to the protection of twelve houses, two apartments, one condominium, and one commercial building. Those numbers were later reaffirmed in a formal letter submitted to the

Erik Scott

LAFD. The numbers don't tell the whole story, but they don't lie either.

Afterward, Matthew reflected on the values that guided him as the fire approached: their mother's influence, their upbringing, their wives, and the expectations they had set for their kids. "What was instilled in us with our mom raising us, and with our wives, with our kids—what we instill in them—of just, 'You're not gonna put anything in front of me that's gonna really scare me off where I'm like, I can't do that.' After what we've been through with the Eaton Fire, there's nothing that's gonna overwhelm me in my decision-making."

~~~~~

Just a few blocks away, another LAFD firefighter was fighting his own battle under the same orange sky.

Darin Lloyd's family had lived in Altadena for eighty years. When the power went out, he ran downstairs, got his pregnant wife to safety, and realized none of his neighbors fully comprehended what was coming. He ran door to door in the dark, trying to warn them.

Driving toward his block, a friend called asking him to check on his home and his dog. When Darin arrived, he saw it: "It literally looked like the whole city was on fire."

Two homes were already fully engulfed in flames. Ninety-mile-per-hour winds were pushing flames toward his own house. He got into his turnouts, ran down the street, and grabbed a residential hose line. "You could feel the heat," he recalled.

A Riverside engine company pulled up and asked where his crew was. "There is no crew," he told them. "There's only me. This is my block."

Neighbors threw him fire extinguishers. He grabbed a shovel and tossed dirt onto burning debris. "I'm praying for anything that might help," he said.

He stayed on the block for four days. Twelve homes were lost. "Altadena is gone," he said. "Seventy percent of it, gone." Childhood landmarks were erased. His grandparents' photographs— lost to fire. "I am thankful I still have a house, but I am torn that so many don't."

Days later, a neighbor approached him with a photograph she had taken during the fire: Darin in his turnouts, standing in her driveway with a hose, spraying water onto her home as flames pushed through the block. It was the first time he realized that someone had captured the moment — the exact moment he had worked to keep her house from burning.

She held the photo out to him with shaking hands, then stepped forward and hugged him, crying. She told him she had lost her husband the year before, and that this house was all she had left. The image she showed him — him defending her home — represented everything that hadn't been taken from her.

"Thank you so much," she said.

For Darin, it crystalized what the chaos hadn't allowed him to see in the moment: that even improvised actions, even working alone with a garden hose, extinguisher, or shovel, could protect something irreplaceable.

"You are needed," he said. "What you do matters."

~~~~~

Moments like these remind us that courage doesn't always look like a full task force on scene—sometimes it's a single firefighter making a stand on their own block. And inside the LAFD, we've

Erik Scott

long had a way of recognizing those rare acts when duty turns into something more.

Long before January 2025, one of my mentors, Battalion Chief Stephen Ruda—the Godfather of PIO, known both for his Italian heritage and for how iconic he was as the department's spokesperson—explained the Los Angeles Fire Department's awards with a line that still circulates in firehouses. "There are four awards we give in this department," he'd say. "The Medal of Valor, the Award of Merit, the Letter of Special Commendation... and a Diet Coke for doing your job." It was classic Ruda: dry humor wrapped around a truth every firefighter understands. Most heroic acts never earn a medal. Sometimes, doing your job under impossible conditions comes with no recognition at all—just the quiet satisfaction of knowing you made a difference.

But some moments rise unmistakably to the level of recognition. A member is entitled to consideration for the Medal of Valor award by performing an act of conspicuous heroism and/or bravery under extreme personal risk above and beyond the calculated personal risk demands of the fire service. A member receiving the Medal of Valor shall also receive a Certificate of Valor, a Medal of Valor Pin, a Resolution of Valor, and have their name inscribed on the Roll of Merit.

Members are entitled to consideration for the Award of Merit for taking conspicuous action in rendering aid during a life-saving or life-threatening situation under circumstances which pose calculated risk to the members, or performing an endeavor which brings significant credit to the Fire Department. A member receiving the Award of Merit shall also receive a Certificate of Merit.

An act performed of unusual character during emergency or non-emergency conditions, requiring initiative or ability worthy of recognition, entitles a member to consideration for a Letter of Special Commendation. Qualifying members shall receive this commendation from the Fire Chief, which may or may not be based on findings by a Board of Honorary Awards.

For their actions at the Eaton Fire—protecting more than a dozen homes under severe conditions—Captain Daniel Lievense and Engineer Matthew Lievense received the Award of Merit.

For his decisive, off-duty stand—evacuating neighbors, defending structures alone until help arrived—Firefighter/Paramedic Darin Lloyd received a Letter of Special Commendation.

None of them fought for a medal. They fought because it was their street, their block, their families, and their neighbors. They fought because they were needed.

Their stories close Part I because they capture the raw reality of those first chaotic days. These were not assignments. These were personal stands on familiar streets. Off duty or on duty, alone or with family, firefighters confronted the flames to protect their communities. What they preserved—homes, memories, and lives—carried Los Angeles onto the long road that followed.

The flames that tore through Altadena, the Pacific Palisades, and several other regions of Los Angeles County left deep scars—charred hillsides, shattered neighborhoods, and families who suddenly had nothing. But in the aftermath of that destruction came a different fight: the slow, complex, emotional work of recovery. Part II begins where the smoke lingers and the questions grow harder—long after the hose lines have been rolled, and when the real healing begins.

A helicopter crew surveys the fire's advancing edge at first light,
providing critical intelligence to guide operations below.
Credit: LAFD AirOps

Erik Scott

A firefighter lowers his head against the intense heat while directing a hose stream beneath a home's eaves, working in close quarters as fire presses in and conditions rapidly deteriorate. Credit: LBFD

Captain Scott briefing California Governor Gavin Newsom and Command Staff at Zuma Base Camp. Credit: CalFire

A light-hearted caricature of the Palisades Fire Logistics Team—
featuring, from left to right, Andrew Ruiz, Rich Moody, and
Thomas Kitahata. Created by Joe Magana

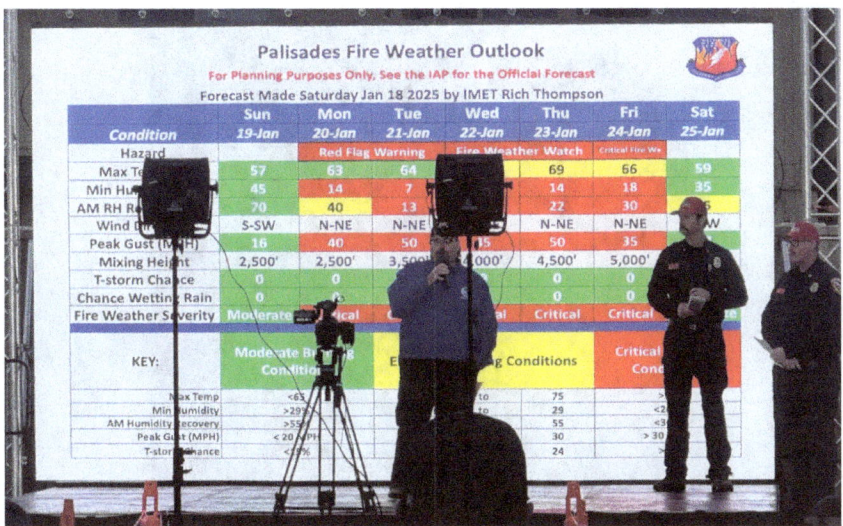

IMET Rich Thompson presents the "Palisades Fire Weather Outlook," outlining upcoming Red Flag and Critical Fire Weather conditions during the operational briefing January 18, 2025. Credit: CalFire

LBFD Community Services staff member Melanie Miller gives a late-night update — a reminder that behind every emergency are dedicated civilian professionals keeping operations running. Credit: LBFD

Erik Scott

*Screen capture of Captain Scott's phone screen January 15, 2025
—one week in. 81 texts. 47 voicemails. 10,481 emails.
The demand for information was immense.*

Calm Amidst Chaos

CNN's Anderson Cooper interviews Jay Leno at the Will Rogers State Beach base camp during the Palisades Fire response. Credit: Erik Scott

Erik Scott

Patty's car, briefly stranded on a boulder along a dirt side road, before firefighters helped guide her safely out. Credit: Patty Philips

Survivor Patty Phillips hugs Captain Malcolm Dicks at the press conference—an emotional reminder that behind every headline is a human story.

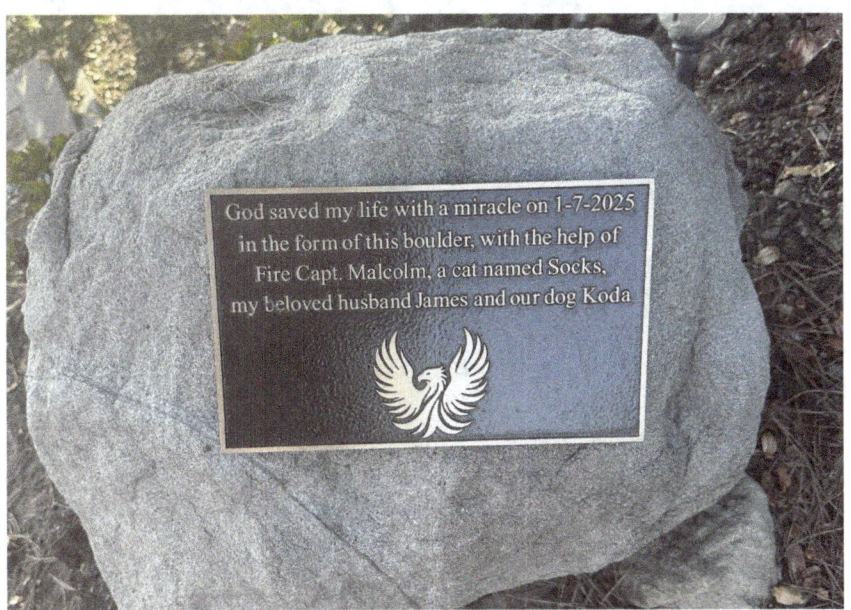

Patty later moved the boulder that saved her life to her property, marking it with a small plaque of gratitude. Credit: Patty Philips

Erik Scott

From left: Erik Scott, Captain Daniel Lievense, Engineer Matthew Lievense, James Lievense, and Firefighter-Paramedic Darin Lloyd on the honor stage at the LAFD Valor event, November 19, 2025.
Credit: KaitLynn Markley

Part 2

RECOVERY, MUDSLIDES, RESILIENCE

Chapter 10

THE LONG TAIL OF RECOVERY

"Resilience isn't abstract. It's choosing to return, to rebuild, and to believe the Palisades will feel like home again."

~ Sue Kohl

When the flames finally released their grip, the work didn't end. It shifted. The firefight gave way to recovery—slower, quieter, but no less demanding.

Returning to the ABC streets and the Pacific Coast Highway (PCH) was different than reporting on them during the fire. Then, it was about describing losses alongside what had been saved. Now, it was about standing with residents as they came back to find nothing left.

I distinctly remember pulling over on PCH and coming across an elderly couple standing in front of the ruins of their home. Their condo had been in the family for more than five decades. Now it was gone—reduced to ash, twisted metal, and fragments of memories.

The husband tried to pick through the rubble while his wife gave me a brief history of the property and how special it had been to their family. I didn't have much to offer that day—no answers that would bring back what they had lost. So I just stood there with them. At one point, I put my arm around her because words didn't feel enough. Later, she wrote to me:

"You listened as we gave you a brief history of the property and how special it was to us and our family, then stood there while my husband tried to pick through the rubble and put your arm around me to comfort me. This, I believe, was probably beyond the scope of your Fire Captain responsibilities but was very much appreciated."

Those words stayed with me, and we stayed in touch. Weeks later, in another note, she told me:

"We still look at the photo of you standing with us, offering comfort. Unfortunately, our little piece of paradise is gone forever... but our lives will never be the same as that condo was in our family for 55 years."

I was humbled when they granted permission to share their story and that photograph. It reminded me that even in uniform, the greatest service sometimes comes not from command posts or press briefings, but from standing quietly with people in their hardest moments and letting them know they're not alone. That photo remains one of the most meaningful posts I've shared on my @PIOErikScott Instagram account. (See photo on page 147.)

Block after block had been reduced to chimneys, each one marking what used to be a home. Cars warped in driveways. Mailboxes stood with no houses behind them. Families picked through ash looking for anything—wedding rings, photographs, keepsakes—that the flames hadn't erased.

These weren't numbers in a briefing anymore. They were people grieving in real time. They often asked us directly what had happened, or why their street was gone while the next still stood. It was raw, and it was painful. But acknowledging the loss honestly was part of recovery.

~~~~~

The ruins weren't just emotional—they were dangerous. Toxic ash, melted synthetic materials, propane tanks, and lithium-ion batteries from electric vehicles all posed risks long after the fire was out.

Many residents, dressed in jeans and sneakers, tried to sift through ruins without realizing what they were breathing or touching. That's why we issued blunt warnings and created flyers posted at checkpoints and recovery centers:

ENTER AT YOUR OWN RISK.
Do not sift through fire debris. Burned homes may contain toxic materials like asbestos, lead, mercury, chemicals, and heavy metals. These hazards can cause lasting health damage— and disturbing debris too soon may even affect insurance claims. Limit your actions to the reasonable recovery of essential items.

It wasn't what survivors wanted to hear, but it was the truth. The danger didn't end when the flames died—it just took a different form.

The weight wasn't only physical. For residents, the loss of a home meant the loss of decades—photographs, heirlooms, the places where families had grown. For firefighters, the images of entire streets reduced to rubble lingered long after the smoke cleared. We fought in grueling conditions—zero visibility, ember storms on every flank, hurricane-force winds that pushed fire faster than crews could catch it. Some areas were simply unwinnable because

Erik Scott

of those winds. The exhaustion, the devastation, the reality of giving everything you had and still watching homes fall—that stays with you.

Fatigue and morale issues didn't come just from the firefight itself, but from returning day after day to destruction. For many, recovery was harder than suppression, because there was no fire left to fight—just the emptiness of what it had taken.

~~~~~

Another survivor of the Palisades fire was Sue Kohl—a longtime resident and successful real estate agent who has lived in the community for more than three decades. For years, she has been both a familiar face in town and a steady voice on the Palisades Community Council, helping organize information and resources for her neighbors.

"I've lived in the Palisades about thirty-two years. I raised five kids there and three step-kids. All went through Palisades schools. It's a tight-knit place—you can't walk through the village without seeing someone you know. My office is with Berkshire Hathaway right in the middle of town, and my house was just four blocks behind Station 69."

On January 7, she and her daughter had just finished their morning office meeting when her daughter stepped outside for coffee, looked up, and ran back in.

"She said, 'Get your stuff—we're going home, we're getting out.' We've done this before. Usually, the fire starts up in the Highlands, Stations 23 and 69 go up, knock it down, we're out a day or two, and back. So we grabbed the dogs and the photo albums—that's our routine—and loaded up."

Neighbors questioned the urgency. "Some said, 'It's going to

Malibu, we'll be fine,' but I told them, 'Do what you think is right. We're leaving.'"

They left around noon, turning east on Sunset toward the 405—just ahead of gridlock that soon stalled cars for miles. "I never had that fear of the fire coming down on me. But farther west, cars were stopped, people abandoning them, embers hitting windshields—it was horrific."

That night, around 7:30 p.m., the block where she lived burned.

"Everything—our house, my office building—gone. Nothing left."

The months that followed tested patience and endurance.

"I had good insurance, and I'm still scared I won't have enough to finish. They make you prove what it would have cost to rebuild the old house—even if you're not rebuilding it exactly the same. My estimator's report was 65 pages. Even the 'loss of use' part—they'd let me spend $40,000 a month if I wanted to, but I'm living in this tiny house in Westchester because it had a yard for the dogs. Not glamorous, just workable."

She's rebuilding—"two stories, windows in, waterproofed"—because indecision felt worse than risk. But she wonders what it will mean to be among the first to return.

"If I'm the only one back for the first six months with no streetlights ... I don't know if I want to be there all alone."

Community connection became survival.

"We've had all these neighborhood groups pop up since the fire, but the one that's really impressive is Team Palisades. They set up a structure—area leads, then block captains—so information flows. I know who my captain is. The alphabet streets have a Monday Zoom at five o'clock every week. There's a huge WhatsApp group; people post, 'Who did you use for debris removal?' or 'Know

Erik Scott

a real-estate lawyer?' It keeps everyone linked. And our block has its own text thread—former neighbors, forever friends. It's amazing. Everybody scattered, but thanks to Zoom and text and email, we still find each other."

She smiles, describing moments that feel normal again. "The Garden Café became our meeting spot when almost nothing else was open. Then CVS reopened and threw a little party—music, everyone invited. And today we had The Longest Table event—two blocks of tables down the street. Everyone brought their own food and sat together. Captain Kitahata was there, too. It was so good to see people just being together again."

Her reflections echoed what many residents later shared in community meetings: the morning's speed and scale made communication difficult in some areas. "Some people didn't realize how quickly things were moving. I remember knocking on my next-door neighbor's door and saying, 'You should get out.'"

She also recalled how fast traffic conditions changed once thousands began leaving at the same time. "It got really busy on Sunset. People were trying to help each other, but there were cars coming from every direction… everyone was doing their best in a very tough situation."

She acknowledged the challenges she experienced but added, "I've met crews who came from up north and showed me houses they saved. People forget how rough it was that day."

She feels empathy, too, for those least able to recover. "Some of my neighbors were underinsured, or their policies got canceled right before the fire. They're having to sell their lots—usually to developers. That's just what's happening. The ones who can rebuild are trying, like my 93-year-old neighbor across the street who's determined to do it."

And she's noticed the way outside help has mattered. "Groups like CORE have been incredible. They helped reopen that senior housing complex at the bottom of Palisades Drive. They've been on the ground doing real work."

When people tell Sue it must be exciting to design a brand-new home, she shakes her head. "No. I loved my old funky house. I loved every inch of it. The thought of a big, beautiful new house doesn't matter—I'd do anything to have the old one back."

That grief lives beside determination. She's practical, forward-looking, and still very much the neighbor who checks on others. "Everybody's trying to be helpful. Even people who weren't that friendly before—everyone's kinder now. We're all in the same boat. I don't think we'll ever forget what happened, but I really believe the Palisades will come back strong."

She believes the timeline will surprise the pessimists. "People say five to ten years … I think that's a lot of hooey. Three years from now, this town's going to be vibrant again. Real estate values will rise, sure, but what matters is that the people come back."

Sue's story captures the heart of recovery—the mixture of heartbreak, realism, and quiet resolve. Her thirty-two years in the Palisades have given her a panoramic view of what was lost and what still binds the community together. Block by block, through Zoom calls, text threads, rebuilt storefronts, and long tables in the street, she and her neighbors are proving that resilience isn't abstract. It's choosing to return, to rebuild, and to believe the Palisades will feel like home again.

~~~~~

Even in the ruins, strength showed through. Neighbors opened their doors to those who had none. Schools and community centers became shelters. Faith groups distributed food, clothing, and water.

Erik Scott

Off-duty firefighters quietly returned to help families sift through debris, standing shoulder-to-shoulder with them.

But recovery stretched beyond neighbors and grassroots groups. Larger volunteer organizations also stepped in, bringing resources and staying power. One of the most visible was CORE— Community Organized Relief Effort.

Co-founded by Sean Penn and led by Ann Young Lee, CORE had already proven itself on a global stage. Lee, who lived in Haiti for seven years after the devastating 2010 earthquake, often says that experience shaped CORE's philosophy: community-powered recovery, led by local voices. With master's degrees in urban planning (NYU) and conflict management (Johns Hopkins), and prior work leading urban response for the UN Secretary General's World Humanitarian Summit, she brought deep expertise to disaster zones around the world—from Pakistan's floods to the wars in Ukraine and Sudan. Under her leadership, CORE grew into a global organization of nearly 300 staff, known for leaning into recovery long after other groups had moved on.

Penn's role has been different but no less important. Best known as an actor and director, he has received two Academy Awards, a Golden Globe, and many other honors. Yet beyond Hollywood, what has defined him is his willingness to show up in the middle of disasters—whether in Haiti, New Orleans, or Los Angeles. In the Palisades, I walked the fire-ravaged streets with Sean and Ann, alongside residents and first responders, hearing them ask, "What else can we do?"—and then watching them do it.

In Los Angeles, their presence was felt immediately. In the days following the Palisades Fire, CORE distributed more than 44,000 items ranging from hygiene kits to N95 masks, provided $2.4 million in direct cash assistance to families, and staffed shelters with charging stations and child-friendly spaces. They also took on harder, less visible work—navigating FEMA paperwork with survivors, providing case managers to guide families for years, and removing hazardous debris when churches, preschools, and small businesses that couldn't afford to start cleanup. In the Palisades alone, they oversaw the safe removal of 92 tons of debris from the Pacific Palisades Presbyterian Church and Preschool, allowing children and staff to return to a vital community hub.

What struck many of us on the ground was CORE's persistence. It's easy for nonprofits to arrive in the spotlight of a disaster and then fade away once the cameras leave. CORE didn't. They leaned forward into recovery—one of the hardest phases to sustain—staying with communities long after the last news crew had packed up.

Their work in Los Angeles became part of a larger story of resilience. On July 24, 2025, CORE and its founders, Sean Penn and Ann Lee, were honored at the Hollywood Reporter's Social Impact Summit, alongside musician and activist John Legend. The event brought together more than 500 leaders from philanthropy, media, and entertainment to spotlight innovative responses to crisis.

I was humbled to be invited to present CORE with the Philanthropic Organization of the Year Award. Standing on stage with Sean and Ann, I shared what it meant to partner with them—first during the COVID-19 pandemic, when Los Angeles needed help with mass testing and vaccinations, and again during the Palisades Fire.

As I said that night, "The most important person on your team is the one who needs help. Lasting change isn't built in a moment—it's built by people who show up again and again to lift others up. That's what Sean and Ann, and the CORE team, embody."

Beyond awards and headlines, I've had the chance to see Ann and Sean in more personal settings. I saw Ann speak at the Lu-

Erik Scott

men Awards in February 2025, where she was honored for CORE's role after the wildfires. She tossed her prepared remarks aside and spoke from the heart, inspiring a room full of changemakers.

I've joined them at a Malibu home where firefighters, county leaders, volunteer departments, heavy equipment operators (Ann has a well-known love for "real-life Tonka toys"), and members of the National Guard gathered. Even in the evenings, Ann and Sean were creating spaces to build relationships that would strengthen recovery. It was powerful to witness and humbling to be a part of.

I've also sat with Sean at his home, drink in hand, as he shared the videos that inspired his philanthropy and showed me his wood-working projects—something he takes on with the same focus and drive he brings to CORE. On another occasion, I joined both Sean and Ann at a restaurant on Sunset Boulevard, seated with attorneys and CORE's CEO, Jérôme Lebleu. Even there, the conversation returned to recovery and the ongoing effort to help people rebuild.

These moments revealed that their leadership wasn't just about stepping in during a crisis—it was about sustaining the work, building connections, and showing up when they were needed most.

Chapter 11

RESILIENCE

"The goal wasn't just to dig. It was to listen."

~ *Bob Bates*

The Palisades Fire was not just a local event but part of a much larger conversation about disaster resilience. It brought together first responders, community volunteers, international non-governmental organizations (NGO), and countless grassroots groups. And it highlighted how rebuilding after a catastrophe isn't just about structures—it's about people. I was deeply impressed by the many volunteer organizations that stepped in to fill the gaps. They deserve a tip of the helmet for showing up when it mattered most.

About a week after the smoke cleared, one familiar face quietly returned to the Palisades—not in uniform, but with open hands and a calm spirit, ready to help his old community begin again.

When retired Los Angeles Fire Captain Bob Bates saw the television footage of the Pacific Palisades engulfed in flame, he felt a twist in his chest. He had spent his last four and a half years at Station 69, serving a community that had come to feel like family. Now, the same streets he once drove for morning patrols were glowing orange under a sky of smoke. "It was disbelief," he recalled. "You know every corner of that place, and suddenly it's unrecognizable."

Bates is a man who carries calm like oxygen. His words come slowly, deliberate, never rushed. There's usually a friendly laugh somewhere in the conversation—quiet, good-natured, the kind that disarms people and makes them want to lean in closer. Talking with him leaves you feeling centered, understood, and, somehow, a little better than when you began.

A week after the fire, Bates returned to the Palisades. This time he wasn't in turnouts or a command vehicle. He came with a small volunteer team working alongside Samaritan's Purse, the international disaster-relief organization known for arriving early and staying late. Their mission was both simple and profound: bring comfort, sift through ashes for mementos, and remind survivors that they weren't alone.

Each morning, hundreds of volunteers gathered at a temporary base in Santa Monica, loading trucks with screen boxes, gloves, and water before caravanning up the winding streets overlooking the Pacific. "The goal wasn't just to dig," Bates said. "It was to listen."

The work uncovered fragments of ordinary life — china plates still patterned with flowers, wedding rings that had been handed down through generations, and even a Los Angeles Rams Super Bowl ring, surprisingly still largely intact inside a collapsed garage. Yet the real restoration happened not in what was recovered, but in the conversations that followed. Residents who had lost everything found themselves surrounded by strangers who treated them like lifelong neighbors.

Bates said the experience reaffirmed a lesson he had learned over decades in uniform—everything comes down to relationships. Whether in leadership, recovery, or daily life, progress begins with listening, caring, and helping one another shoulder the weight.

"Anybody can do physical work," Bates said. "What matters is showing up, caring, and staying connected after the headlines fade."

Before the Palisades Fire, Bates had already traveled to Hawaii and North Carolina to assist in disaster relief operations—experiences that shaped his perspective on what true recovery looks like. So when tragedy struck closer to home, his instinct was immediate: to return, to listen, and to serve.

"Everywhere you go," he said, "you find the same thing. People need to be heard. They need to know someone still cares."

In Bob Bates's calm voice and quiet presence, the spirit of the Palisades found a mirror—steady, compassionate, and unbroken.

~~~~~

That same quiet strength rippled throughout the community in unexpected ways. In living rooms, classrooms, and newsrooms, people found new meaning in connection. KTLA anchor Courtney Friel— a journalist charged with telling the story and a mother keeping her children safe—felt that pull deeply. For her, resilience began not with rebuilding walls, but with rebuilding relationships

On January 7, she was standing in line at Paul Revere Middle School to pick up her children after the evacuation order. "I was setting up phoners for KTLA while watching the live stream with people who thought they might lose their homes," she recalled. "It was surreal—one part of me was Mom in the pickup line, the other part was a reporter already on assignment."

That night, she anchored coverage until 4:00 a.m., while her ex-husband and his wife, fellow journalist Lauren Lyster, defended their Palisades home with garden hoses. Against the odds, they saved it, even as most of their street was reduced to ash.

Erik Scott

The next morning, Courtney walked through neighborhoods with a list of homes to check for friends and neighbors. Seven of the nine were gone. "I know at least 20 people who lost their homes," she said. "I've covered many wildfires over the years, but this was the craziest thing I've ever seen."

The fire's reach touched every corner of her life. Her daughter's former school was destroyed. Her son's classes were relocated to the old Sears building while Palisades High remained closed. Her children couldn't return to their father's house, badly damaged by smoke, and they had to replace most of their belongings. Still, she kept reporting—telling the stories of families who lost everything, even following survivors into the aftermath of the Eaton Fire weeks later.

For Courtney, the boundaries between professional and personal collapsed. She was a mother housing her displaced family, a neighbor grieving with her community, and a reporter responsible for capturing it all. "It was so intense," she said. "Traumatic, yes—but also a reminder of how much community matters when everything else is stripped away."

~~~~~

But resilience wasn't just found in the community—it had to be lived inside the fire service, too. Some of our own firefighters returned from the front lines to discover their homes gone. It's a strange, humbling reversal. We are trained to protect, to be the helpers, the ones people look to when disaster strikes. Yet the Palisades and Eaton Fires reminded us that nature doesn't draw those lines. Some of my colleagues—men I see in the locker room nearly every day—became survivors themselves. Firefighters—those who spent their days and nights protecting strangers' homes—returned to find their own consumed by flames. Here are two of their stories.

~~~~~

When the January 2025 Eaton Fire erupted under fierce Santa Ana winds, it wasn't only the hillsides that burned—it was homes, memories, and the fragile sense of safety for countless families. Among those who lost everything was Captain Gerardo "Jerry" Puga, a veteran Los Angeles firefighter whose own neighborhood was consumed overnight.

What makes Jerry's story remarkable isn't the destruction— it's the resilience that followed. In the days after the fire, he turned his loss into action, helping neighbors defend their homes and finding strength through the Widows, Orphans & Disabled Firefighters Fund, a lifeline for those who have given everything in service to others.

What follows is Jerry's story—in his own words.

"It started around seven or eight o'clock that night. Someone—I honestly don't even remember who—told me there was a fire that had broken out in Eaton. We're a family of five: my wife, my daughter, her boyfriend, my son, and me. We went to the window and could see the fire up in the hills. Because of the wind, my wife was nervous. She asked, 'Should we leave the house? Should we evacuate?' I told her, 'No, we're far from the mountains. The fire's to the east, and the wind's blowing east—away from us. We're safe.'

Not long after that, the power went out. With no lights, no news, nothing to do, I said, 'Let's just go to bed. We'll see what's going on in the morning.'

Around three in the morning, I woke up to the smell of smoke. Something didn't feel right. I told my wife, 'I'm going to take a quick drive, just to check on things.' I got in the car and drove east—toward where I thought the fire had been. That's when I first saw it up close: houses already burning, embers flying sideways, raining down in sheets. The wind had shifted, and it was blowing everything straight toward our neighborhood.

I called my wife immediately. 'Get up. Get our daughter. Get in the car and leave — now.'

By the time I got back, the fire was moving fast. My son and I looked over and saw our neighbor's house already engulfed in flames. That was the trigger point. I knew there was no way two garden hoses were going to stop what was coming. I told him, 'We've got to go. Get in the car.'

Visibility was near zero. Smoke everywhere. Couldn't see five feet ahead. Luckily, no one else was on the road, so we just drove, heading toward Pasadena until we finally reached clearer air. We parked, waited for the winds to die down, and said we'd circle back once things calmed.

When we returned about an hour later, our home was completely engulfed in flames.

There was nothing we could do.

A few hours later, after sunrise, we came back again — hoping maybe, somehow, something had changed. But there was nothing left. The house was gone. We started driving around, checking on neighbors, looking for anyone who needed help. We found one home that was about to catch — flames from the next house were spreading through the bushes. So we stopped. Others stopped too. People showed up with shovels, hoses, anything they could find. Together we cleared brush, cut away fuel, did whatever we could until an engine company arrived. That spirit — neighbors helping neighbors in the middle of chaos — stayed with me.

For days after, I kept going back to the property. I think part of me believed it was a bad dream — that maybe the next morning I'd wake up and the house would still be standing. But three or four days later, it finally sank in. This was real. Everything we owned was gone.

Then came something just as powerful as the fire itself: the response. The calls started coming from our union, UFLAC Local 112, from the Los Angeles Firemen's Relief Association, from friends across the department—checking in, asking what we needed. The Widows, Orphans & Disabled Firefighters Fund showed up almost immediately with support packages and gift cards. Honestly, at that point, I didn't even know what to ask for. We had nothing but the clothes on our backs. Their compassion filled a void that words can't.

That kind of care—having people call every day, making sure your family's okay—reminds you what brotherhood and sisterhood really mean in this job. It's humbling. It keeps you moving forward when everything around you is gone.

Now, my focus is on recovery. I told my family, 'We're not looking in the rearview mirror anymore. Only through the windshield.' What's behind us is gone—but what's ahead still matters. The fire took our home, but it didn't take our hope."

In a profession built on saving others, losing everything yourself is an unthinkable test of perspective. Yet Jerry met that moment with the same courage he's shown his entire career—calm under pressure, compassion in action, and a belief that service doesn't stop when the uniform comes off.

His story mirrors what so many firefighter families faced after the Altadena Fire: devastation met with grace, despair met with purpose. Through the Relief Association and the Widows, Orphans & Disabled Firefighters Fund, hope arrived in the form of human connection—reminding us that recovery isn't just about rebuilding homes but restoring hearts.

Jerry's words embody the spirit of this section: that even when the flames take everything tangible, resilience is what remains.

~~~~~

Another colleague and friend, John, is a well-respected inspector in our legal division. I see him nearly every day in the locker room. He's what we call a "locker room leader"—the kind of presence you can't miss, and one you actually feel the absence of when he's not there. Fun, funny, respectful—and beneath the hard shell, a loving husband and loyal friend.

John and his wife, Monica, lived in Altadena. Their dream home of seventeen years sat in the path of the Eaton Fire. As flames closed in, he rushed back from duty to evacuate his wife and their dog, pounding on his neighbors' doors—including an elderly couple—to get them out safely. Then, with three garden hoses, he stayed behind in a desperate stand. Visibility was near zero, the winds so strong they knocked him from a ladder as he tried to douse embers. He crashed to the ground, injuring his knees. He also suffered smoke inhalation and burns to his face before finally being forced to retreat.

In the days that followed, he sifted through ash and twisted metal, pointing out where the bed used to be, where his dresser once stood. Some fragments could be salvaged—family photos from the 1920s and 30s, pieces of his grandmother's china. But so much was gone. He told me the hardest part was literally throwing his hands up, realizing he had to walk away from the house he and Monica had worked tirelessly to shape into their dream home.

As if the fire's destruction weren't enough, looters struck the ruins before he could return, prying into safes and cabinets. That violation deepened the wound.

Monica later told reporters that in the middle of all this, her simple message was: "I wish we had more resources." She wasn't blaming, she was speaking from the raw pain of seeing their home and neighborhood destroyed.

At first, she wasn't sure she could rebuild. The trauma was that deep. In the end, they chose to, but recovery will take years.

My wife and I spent time with them off-duty, hearing about the million little battles they faced—insurance disputes, FEMA paperwork, temporary housing. It was like death by a thousand paper cuts. Suddenly, this proud firefighter—my friend—was navigating the same maze of loss as the very people we usually serve.

And yet, even amid that, John still showed up for work. Still put on the uniform. Still carried himself as the tough firefighter he's always been. One night, bandages still on his face, he was honored as the "Hero of the Game" at a Kings hockey match. The crowd saw a man who had given his all for his community. I saw my friend, still carrying scars, still leading by example.

Support eventually found him, too. The Los Angeles Firemen's Relief Association stepped up in a major way, providing financial and emotional assistance not just to John but to many firefighters who lost their homes. SoCal Honda even surprised him with a new car to ease the burden of starting over. John often tells me that once things settle down, he wants to join LAFRA himself—to give back to the same brotherhood that carried him when he needed it most.

For firefighters, losing your home is an awkward, unnatural reversal. We're used to being the helpers, not the ones needing help. But John's story reminded all of us: disaster doesn't discriminate. And strength isn't just something we encourage in others— it's something we sometimes have to draw on ourselves.

~~~~~

Courtney, Jerry, and John's experiences echoed what many fire victims were living: survival, loss, and resilience unfolding at the same time. Out of that struggle, grassroots efforts began to emerge.

One strong example of that resilience was embodied in Larry Vein, known throughout the Palisades as Pali Strong. Midway

Erik Scott

through our deployment at Will Rogers State Beach, his name kept surfacing among PIOs. He wasn't a reporter, but he had quickly become a trusted voice in the community—sharing vetted updates, amplifying official guidance, and striving to keep his neighbors calm and informed.

I still remember the knock on my trailer door: "Sorry to bother you sir, but Larry Vein would really like to speak with you." I stepped outside, and that moment began a partnership built on mutual respect. Larry wasn't looking for credit; he wanted to help. His presence reminded us that trusted messengers weren't only inside the command post—they were also in the neighborhoods, carrying information where we couldn't always reach.

Months later, when the Getty Villa reopened on June 27, 2025, after nearly six months of closure and repair, it felt right that Larry should be there. The fire had blackened the grounds and threatened priceless collections, but crews accomplished an extraordinary recovery effort:

- Fire-damaged grounds were deep-cleaned
- Water and HVAC systems were flushed
- Over 1,300 trees were removed

Amazingly, the Villa's interior remained intact—protected by both its design and the outstanding efforts of firefighters who had defended the site at the height of the fire.

The Getty invited first responders to the reopening, and I personally recommended that Larry be included—not just as a guest, but as a community partner whose efforts deserved recognition. They agreed wholeheartedly. That day, surrounded by the restored gardens and art, Larry presented me with a medal and ribbon. I wore it with pride, not for myself, but as a reflection of the community's gratitude and determination to move forward.

That photograph—me standing beside Larry with the medal around my neck and the Villa gleaming behind us—captures more than an event. It symbolizes the strength of a community that refused to break, and the partnerships that carried us not only through the fire but through the long, difficult road of recovery.

Erik Scott

Chapter 12

THE NEIGHBORHOOD CHIEF

"Pray for the Palisades"

~ Chief Deputy Joseph Everett

Chief Deputy Joseph Everett wasn't just the Incident Commander of the Palisades Fire—he grew up in nearby Malibu, but his family's roots ran deep in the Palisades, the community where generations of Everetts had served and lived. He was born and raised along the Malibu coast, the son and grandson of firefighters who had worn the badge before him. His childhood was spent exploring the same canyons and ridges that, decades later, would test every ounce of his leadership. In the Everett family, the fire service wasn't just a profession—it was a legacy.

He often described that connection as both a privilege and a burden. "It hurt," he said. "It hurt bad. I felt like a neighborhood chief. I told them, I'm your guy. I've got your back."

That sense of responsibility ran deep. The Malibu and Pacific Palisades communities weren't lines on a map for him—they were home. He knew their topography, their weather patterns, and their vulnerabilities. He'd fought fires here before, trained here, and watched his friends raise families here. When the Palisades Fire began, Everett felt it personally. He carried the weight not just of command, but of belonging.

In the days before ignition, Everett and neighboring chiefs were already on high alert. He coordinated closely with regional partners, including Deputy Chief Tom Clemo of the Santa Monica Fire Department and Assistant Chief Zipperman of the Beverly Hills Fire Department, confirming that their strike teams could deploy within minutes.

When the Hollywood Hills Sunset Fire broke first, Everett took command and stabilized the incident. Crews were still working hotspots when radio traffic came in about a new start in the Palisades—one with far greater potential. He immediately recognized the difference. "I freed everything I could," Everett recalled. "Gave Battalion 5 back their resources so they could keep mopping up Sunset, and told Clemo, get a strike team moving to 23's—now."

It was a calculated decision that reflected his instincts as both a tactician and a local. He could feel where the next battle was headed.

He understood the terrain intimately. As we spoke, I was struck by how systematically he named each street, knowing their layout, slope, and exposure from memory. "I've driven those roads my whole life."

By the time Everett reached the coast, the Palisades Fire had turned into a roaring wall of flame. Winds howled through the canyons at speeds few firefighters ever face. "They weren't just embers," he said. "They were pieces of two-by-fours ripping through the air."

Within hours, there were roughly 25 firefighter emergencies. Some involved momentary disorientation or lost contact—a firefighter calling out that they couldn't find their captain. Others were injuries or smoke-related distress. A few escalated into full firefighter emergencies. Amid the chaos, Everett contacted Battalion Chief

Conroy with a clear directive. "Don't be afraid to send ambulances in for rescues," he said.

He wasn't speaking only about firefighters—anyone in distress who needed help. Conroy's reply was immediate: "I've been doing that for two hours, sir."

Evacuations were nonstop.

"There were a lot of ambulances that night," Everett remembered. He credited the coordination among first responders who worked to move people out of harm's way as conditions deteriorated. Roads were choked with smoke and debris; visibility was almost zero. Crews had to navigate narrow streets and steep grades while the wind screamed through the canyons.

One of the most significant incidents unfolded near the top of Palisades Drive, where Captain Hernandez and his crew discovered an assisted-living facility in immediate danger. The building housed more than 20 residents, many elderly or unable to walk. Flames were cresting the hillside above them when the crew arrived. Hernandez quickly organized a corridor for evacuation, calling for additional ambulances and using nearby engines to shield the structure long enough to move people out.

"They were literally carrying people through smoke and wind," Everett said. "It wasn't just a rescue—it was leadership and compassion in action."

As residents were brought down the hill, ambulances and rescue units staged along Palisades Drive and Sunset Boulevard. The medical group at Will Rogers coordinated their triage and transport to nearby hospitals, while other units returned uphill to check for stragglers. The operation continued for more than an hour under gusts strong enough to rock the rigs in place.

"That's what impressed me," Everett said. "Nobody quit. Those guys didn't wait for orders—they saw a need and they acted.

Erik Scott

That's who we are."

He later described the Palisades Drive evacuation as one of the clearest examples of the night's dual themes: command and compassion, running side by side under impossible conditions.

At the same time, Everett was directing resources toward another priority—the protection of key cultural and infrastructure sites, including the Getty Villa. Perched along Pacific Coast Highway at the mouth of the canyon, the Getty Villa houses ancient Greek, Roman, and Etruscan art and is one of Los Angeles's most treasured museums. "They've got art older than Christ," Everett said. "We made sure we didn't lose that."

He assigned a handful of engines and patrol units to protect the site, coordinating closely with law enforcement to maintain access on the narrow stretch of highway. The Villa's location—surrounded by vegetation on steep terrain above the ocean—made it uniquely vulnerable to ember cast from the canyon winds. Crews positioned along the perimeter kept watch through the night, using hose lines and water streams to cool hotspots and knock down spot fires blown across the ridgeline.

"The fire was pushing hard out of the canyons," Everett recalled. "We had resources staged along the highway and at the Villa itself, ready for ember wash." The combination of those preparations, the site's defensible construction, and a gradual wind shift spared the museum. "If we'd lost the Getty Villa, that would've been a loss felt around the world," he said.

Against tremendous odds, the Villa remained untouched—a moment of pride and relief amid an otherwise punishing night.

Not long after, new reports came from Carbon Canyon. Civilians with burn injuries were being treated near the coastline, and conditions were too volatile for standard engines to reach the area safely. Everett drew on an old part of himself—his years as an ocean lifeguard with Los Angeles County. He understood what those men and women could do and how well they knew that stretch of coast.

"I told them to put on their brush gear, take their four-wheel-drive trucks, and go," he said. "I knew them all from my time as a lifeguard, and I trusted them."

The request was unconventional but practical. The lifeguards were trained in rescue and emergency medical care, and their trucks were built for the kind of terrain where fire engines bogged down. They moved quickly toward the scene, navigating through smoke and ash that rolled down the canyons toward the water. "They went without hesitation," Everett said.

It was another example of cross-agency trust born from experience. Everett's familiarity with both worlds—firefighting and lifeguarding—made that coordination possible. The decision bridged two disciplines and likely saved lives.

As the fire advanced, Everett felt the tug-of-war between tactical logic and human instinct. "The compassion and empathy—they're in firefighters, even when we don't see it," he said. "Almost to a fault. They didn't want to lose those houses. They didn't want to lose that battle for the people who lived there." He added, "You can't take compassion out of a firefighter."

The situation on the ground was chaotic. "If I had ten reservoirs, it still would've been a problem," Everett said. Water supply, wind, terrain—everything was working against them. Crews came off the line exhausted, streaked with soot, their gear shredded from embers and heat. "They were beaten up," Everett said. "But it never ceased to amaze me how great they were."

He recalled one young firefighter whose face was raw from exposure. "It looked like someone had taken sandpaper to his cheeks," Everett said. "He wasn't going home. I told him, take care of yourself. Be careful."

Erik Scott

By the next morning, many of those same firefighters were back at the line. During the 7:00 a.m. briefing, Everett looked out across hundreds of faces and tried to give them something more than assignments. "What I saw were people who refused to quit," he said later. "That's a testament to who they are—hard battles fought by hard people."

For Everett, leadership that week wasn't about rank or authority—it was about empathy. "They were fighting for their neighbors," he said. "And when you see that, you realize this job is about people, not property."

By nightfall, the incident had drawn near-constant media coverage. Crews from across Los Angeles crowded the coastal staging areas, lights cutting through the smoke. Among them was NBC's Robert Kovacik, who caught Everett on camera with the hills behind him glowing orange.

"Pray for the Palisades," Everett said as the live shot ended. The simple, unscripted phrase struck a chord. Within hours, it was replayed across networks and shared widely on social media—an image of calm and conviction amid chaos.

At home, his wife saw the broadcast and later told him how proud she was to see him representing their community. But Everett remembered it differently. "It just felt so awful," he said quietly. "I didn't fail," he added. "But I didn't win either."

Earlier at the command post, a woman Everett had known for years approached him in tears. She wasn't a firefighter—she was a community volunteer. She hugged him tightly, shaking. "It's going to be OK," he told her.

Months later, around February, she texted him during a concert, attaching a photo of herself with friends. Her message read, Can you feel the love? Everett said he never forgot it. "She's always kind of been my barometer for how the public feels," he explained.

The sentiment wasn't always positive—at times, it shifted, reflecting the public's own emotional swing between gratitude and grief.

He refused to leave. "This was my home," he said. "My neighborhood. It was on my shoulders. I wasn't leaving." The weight of that statement was clear. For Everett, leadership wasn't optional—it was inherited.

"It was mental anguish," he said. "You feel the pressure from every direction—your people, the public, and the fire itself."

When I heard him say that, it struck a deep chord. During my own 28 day deployment, I'd felt that same pressure—the constant pull between serving the firefighters beside me, the public counting on information, and the incident itself that never seemed to rest. Even after returning home, through media interviews and community events that followed, including the award shows, that weight lingered. Everett's words captured what so many of us had felt but rarely said aloud.

That pressure didn't ease when the flames died down. In the days that followed, Everett began to measure progress in what he called minor victories. "When I was a captain, three houses were about what you could handle," he said. "That night, if we saved three, that was a win."

In hurricane-force winds and conditions that repeatedly bordered on unworkable, defending even a handful of homes required enormous effort and an unwavering commitment to hold the line. Each small success mattered. "You focus on what you can hold and move on," he said. "In the end, we weren't fighting for structures— we were fighting for the people who lived behind them.

That kind of weight couldn't be carried alone. Everett often said that every large-scale incident depends on the quiet professionals who keep it moving—the ones who solve problems no one sees. He praised Captains Andrew Ruiz, Thomas Kitahata, and Richard

Moody, who managed logistics under extraordinary pressure.

"The logistical work they did was incredible," Everett said. "They found hotels that donated rooms for firefighters who hadn't seen their families in weeks. They looked out for us."

One of them even asked him, When's the last time you saw your wife?

"About 15 days ago," Everett replied. They arranged a brief overnight stay so he could see her. "That was leadership too," he said. "Looking out for each other."

Through the exhaustion came one bright memory. His son Jack, a Los Angeles County lifeguard and environmental-science student at the University of Redlands, had seen the emergency-hire notice and wanted to help.

"At first, I told him to stay at school," Everett said. Then he reconsidered. "I called him back and said, talk to your professors, tell them what's going on." Jack's professors encouraged him to go. Within hours, he was driving home.

"A few hours later, I looked up and there he was," Everett said. "Walking up in Blundstones, jeans, and a canvas jacket. He looked like Jack Ryan."

The next morning, Everett stood before more than a thousand responders at the 7:00 a.m. Operations Briefing. Jack stood in the crowd watching his father lead. "That's the legacy," Everett said. "That's the good part."

Jack spent the following week helping at the command post— sorting donations, fueling vehicles, and assisting with mapping in the GIS unit. The University of Redlands later profiled him for his service.

Chapter 13

AFTER THE FIRE, RECOVERY AND THE RAINS

"I'm not going to die in this car today."

~ *Fire Inspector II Jerry Kao*

Public messaging shifted almost overnight—moving from wildfire evacuations to new evacuations for potential mudslides and debris flows, along with guidance on sandbags, erosion control, and reminders to stay clear during storms.

The process of rebuilding was long and tangled. Insurance claims, FEMA paperwork, city permits, and hazardous material removal all moved slower than most residents hoped. At community meetings, emotions ran high.

Our role wasn't to lead those recovery meetings or manage the long tail of the disaster. The fire department is fully engaged during the prevention, response, and mitigation phases—but once an incident moves into recovery, city, county, state, and federal partners take the lead. While we addressed immediate hazardous-materials concerns, the longer-term recovery work—comprehensive fire debris removal, additional hazardous-materials testing, permitting, and restoration—transitioned to city, county, state, and federal partners. As they took the lead, we began demobilizing and returning to our primary mission: responding to new emergencies across Los Angeles.

Still, during those first days after the fire, we remained closely connected to the community. We listened to residents' concerns, understood their frustration, and answered what we could before handing off to the agencies responsible for the next phase. People didn't just want information—they wanted acknowledgment of how hard it all was. Sometimes, the most meaningful thing we could offer was clarity, empathy, and a bridge to the partners carrying recovery forward.

Simply put, we saw both sides. On the fire ground, we heard residents' anger, grief, and frustration about hazardous-material cleanup and debris removal. At the same time, we saw recovery teams working nonstop, pushing through barriers and moving more quickly than many realized in the moment. Standing in that middle space, we understood why survivors felt every day was too slow—and we could also see that progress, while imperfect, was advancing steadily.

Not all residents were satisfied with the pace. Some felt every step took too long, every requirement too burdensome. That frustration was real—and understandable. When you've lost everything, even one more week feels like forever.

City leadership also highlighted the historic pace of recovery, compared to other devastating California wildfires, and the preparation for upcoming rain in a May 19, 2025, post titled "L.A.'s Disaster Recovery Effort on Track to be Fastest in Modern California History." It read:

> "Nearly 900,000 tons of debris have been removed from the Palisades area. To date, 54 permits for 40 addresses have been issued related to rebuilding efforts and

hundreds of applications are in the process of being reviewed. The first permit was issued 57 days after the start of the Palisades Fire, more than twice as fast as permits were issued after the devastating Camp and Woolsey fires.

Fastest Hazardous Materials Clearing in EPA History: Phase 1 of the debris removal finished in 28 days – months ahead of expectations – and removed more than 300 tons of hazardous materials, such as exploded lithium-ion batteries, from the Palisades.

Debris Removal Moving at Historic Pace: In coordination with the County, Phase 2 of the debris removal process is well underway and began just 35 days after the fires ignited — roughly half the time it took after the devastating 2018 Woolsey Fire.

Construction Underway across the Palisades: To date, 54 permits for 40 addresses related to rebuilding efforts have been issued for projects in the Palisades. Hundreds of permit applications are in the process of being reviewed.

Utilities Restored at Record Rate: In just two months, water and power were safely restored for standing homes in the Palisades. In comparison, safe drinking water wasn't restored until 18 months after the devastating Camp Fire in Paradise, California.

Reinforced Burn Areas Prone to Slides: The City

shored up burn areas ahead of wet weather this season by urgently installing more than 13,500 feet of concrete barriers and laying down more than 7,500 sandbags."

The reality was that both things could be true: residents were hurting and anxious to move forward—and at the same time, recovery actions in Los Angeles were advancing more quickly than it may have appeared at the time.

~~~~~

For firefighters, recovery also meant confronting what couldn't be saved. Some carried guilt. Others carried exhaustion. But we reminded each other of a truth: thousands of lives were evacuated safely, thousands of homes were held, and the response adapted to unprecedented conditions. That mattered—it helped us carry the weight forward.

The recovery phase underscored a hard truth: the fire may be out, but its impact lingers. Clearing toxic debris, supporting survivors, making homes more resistant to wildfire, and preparing for mudslides all became part of the mission.

Progress can be slow. But step by step, resilience grew stronger than loss. And that was the story worth telling—because recovery, as hard as it was, showed that Los Angeles wasn't broken.

But recovery wasn't the end of the story.

~~~~~

The fires of January had barely cooled when the skies opened again—this time with water instead of hurricane winds and flame. On February 13, 2025, a powerful storm swept through Los Angeles, hammering the same scarred hillsides that had burned only weeks earlier. The earth, stripped of its roots, gave way. The water turned to mud, and the mud began to move.

As rivers of debris rushed toward the coast, our team was once again deployed into the same war zone we'd just left. Captain Adam Van Gerpen, firefighter David Ortiz, and I were sent back into the burn scar to coordinate safety messaging and field operations. News crews were already there when we arrived, capturing the renewed threat to a community that had barely begun to recover.

The fire had been a brutal fight that knocked us to our knees. The storm was the kick to the gut that came before we could stand back up.

That morning, one of our own—Fire Inspector II Jerry Kao— was driving north on Pacific Coast Highway, the ocean stretching out to his left and the steep, burned hillside rising hard to his right. Rain tapped against the windshield as he crept through the scarred landscape, reassessing damaged hydrant access points along the way. The drive was familiar—slow, careful, shadowing a pair of contractor trucks as they crawled through the scarred terrain. The rain was steady, and visibility was low. "We were doing maybe 20 miles per hour," he recalled. "Four miles of slow rolling, watching the road, making sure we stayed clear of any slides." Moments later, the hillside above him gave way.

Then, just north of Tuna Canyon, traffic paused. A truck ahead merged. Kao eased forward at barely five miles per hour.

Without warning, the hillside let go. "A debris flow formed out of nowhere," he said. "I never even saw it start. It came up and over the roadway and slammed into the passenger side of my car. The force was unbelievable—it shoved me across all three lanes. I knew immediately I was going over the edge."

In that split second, there was no time to radio a Mayday, no

Erik Scott

time to think of protocol. The world tilted and fell away. The Chevrolet tumbled backward down the slope, glass and metal shattering around him. "I remember being angry," he said quietly. "Angry that I had no control, that I might leave my wife and kids behind."

Inside the cab, airbags deployed with a violent rush, wrapping him in a cocoon of fabric and noise. Mud pressed across the windows as debris flow dragged the vehicle downhill. Rocks pounded the frame. The car came to rest on the beach, tilted on its side. For a moment—silence.

"I told myself out loud, 'I'm not going to die in this car today.' I didn't have any control over what happened next but saying it gave me something to hold onto. I knew no one could get to me. I had to get myself out."

He waited, listening. The debris flow still roared nearby, but the vehicle had finally stopped shifting. Cautiously, he drew his knife, slashed through the side curtain airbags, and pulled them aside. Light seeped through the muddy glass. He forced the driver's door—packed tight with mud—until it gave way.

"The second I stepped out, I sank past my knees," he said. "It was thick, heavy, cold. I just remember thinking, Move. Get out of the flow."

He clawed his way toward the base of the cliff, then started climbing—hand over hand, through slick earth and brush, over fences, up toward the highway above. His department radio was gone, swallowed by the mud. When he finally reached the top, soaked and bleeding from a shallow cut on his arm, he pulled out his cell phone.

The first call was to dispatch, confirming what had just happened: vehicle down, firefighter self-extricated, no additional victims.

The second was the one he dreaded. "The hardest call was

to my wife," he said. "She's lived through the same stress I have—probably more. I didn't want to bring that kind of fear home again."

Minutes later, CHP officers reached him and guided him to safety. A passerby's video of the aftermath—Kao climbing calmly up the embankment, mud-covered but steady—circulated online. To the public, it looked like composure. To his colleagues, it was survival.

At the hospital, he was treated for minor abrasions and released back to duty. The physical recovery was quick; the mental one took longer.

He thought often about how close it had been—how another few feet or a different angle might have ended his story entirely.

"I'm not special," he insisted. "Any firefighter in my shoes would've done the same thing. Our training teaches us to suppress the panic and focus on the next step—get to A, then B, then C. But afterward, when you go home, you realize your family didn't sign up for that kind of risk. And that's what stays with you."

These days, when he drops his daughter off at school, he sometimes catches himself replaying that morning. The rain. The hillside. The impact. The climb. Then he looks in the rearview mirror and sees his daughter smiling—and he's reminded why he fought so hard to get out of that car.

"I'm just grateful," he said. "Grateful that I got to make that second call and come home."

~~~~~

Driving the coast after the storm, I passed Duke's Malibu—the well-known restaurant on Pacific Coast Highway that pays tribute to the early days of surfing in Malibu and had survived the Palisades Fire, just as it had the Woolsey and Franklin fires. I remember think-

Erik Scott

ing they must have felt lucky. And then the rains came. Mud tore through the beloved restaurant, leaving scars of a different kind. My heart sank. Survive the fire, then get hit by the flood.

That was the story across Southern California. You could be spared by the fires but fall victim to the mudslides.

That same week, I found myself standing with a group of reporters along Pacific Coast Highway. Water was already carving channels down the hillside. My training told me what came next. The ground was hydrophobic from the burn, stripped of roots and foliage, rain hammering directly into the soil. I rolled through mental slides of past mudflows, and the hairs on the back of my neck stood up. That slope was going to give way.

I pointed out what I was seeing—the rills, the flow, the steep grade—shared past examples and told them plainly it wasn't safe. I couldn't force them to leave, but I told them I was leaving and suggested they move up the road.

Matt Gutman, a well-known national correspondent for ABC News and someone I've gotten to know over the years, was among them. He recognized the danger, too, and later texted me:

Matt: "Erik—that spot where we were— wasn't that Big Rock? You literally called it—the danger there."

Erik: "Agreed. That area really worried me. Please be safe out there, my friend."

Matt: "We will—and we got out of there thanks to you. Thanks again and stay safe."

It was a profound reminder that PIOs aren't just responsible for keeping the public safe—we also look out for the safety of the press, who often work shoulder to shoulder with us at emergency scenes to keep millions informed.

~~~~~

Mudslides don't happen every time it rains. They depend on two things: rate and duration. If the rain comes slow and steady, Mother Earth acts like a sponge and absorbs it. But when it falls heavy and fast, she can't keep up.

After a wildfire, the risk multiplies. Burn scars leave soil hydrophobic—water-repellent instead of absorbent. Without roots to hold it or foliage to slow the drops, rain hits hard, runs fast, and turns slopes into rivers of mud.

After standing in both disasters—the fire in January and the mudslides in February—I couldn't help but think: if only.

If the rain had come first, relative humidity would have been high, and the fire would have been far slower and far less catastrophic. If the wind hadn't howled first, followed by storms weeks later, the story would have been drastically different. Instead, Mother Nature gave us windstorms first, then rain on bare, scarred hillsides. If only it had been the other way around.

That's the hard truth of disaster work: we can't bargain with nature. We adapt, we warn, we fight, and we endure.

Erik Scott

Chapter 14

THE WEIGHT WE CARRY

"The Palisades Fire was not just another deployment.
It left scars—on lungs, on minds, and on hearts—that would
take far longer to heal than the land itself."

~ *Erik Scott*

For most of the public who didn't lose their home, the fire ended when the last flame was out. For firefighters, it didn't. The Palisades Fire lived on in memories, in bodies worn thin, and in the invisible weight it left behind.

On January 22, 2025—fifteen days into the firestorm—a new fire broke out north of Los Angeles: the Hughes Fire.

At 10:42 a.m., a column of smoke was caught on the Burnt Peak ALERTCalifornia camera. Within minutes, it had a name. By 10:50 a.m., engines reported a rapid rate of spread with heavy spotting. At 11:00 a.m., Incident Command requested fifty engines, ten strike teams, ten hand crews, and a dozen water tenders—an urgent reinforcement that told us how quickly this fire was escalating.

And for the first time, the crisis became personal. My parents lived in the path of that fire. I got word almost immediately and called them to evacuate. That decision spared them the chaos of a last-minute scramble, but it didn't spare me the fear of knowing they were on the road as flames advanced.

In my trailer at the command post, I had maps open, wind data pulled up, fire history layers displayed, and my mom's live location on my phone—trying to guide them out safely. They eventually reached the 126 highway, but in that hour, I wasn't a spokesperson or a PIO. I was a son.

When the call ended, I closed the trailer door and let the weight break through. For the first time, exhaustion, stress, and fear for my own family all collided and I got choked up. Then I straightened my uniform and went back to work. There were still press briefings to deliver, updates to push, and a public counting on calm.

That moment reminded me of something important: leadership under pressure is one thing. Leadership when your own family is in the line of fire is another. It showed me that beneath the uniforms, we're all human—carrying the same fears as the people we serve.

~~~~~

As the deployment stretched on, the toll became harder to ignore. Toward the end, I developed a cough that wouldn't go away. My voice, already strained from constant briefings, was fraying. Even when I tried to rest, the smoke was inescapable.

When we finally demobilized on Day 28, I went to the doctor. Two physicians listened to my lungs, and both heard the same thing: persistent wheezing. Chest X-rays followed. I was prescribed albuterol to open the lungs, benzonatate for the cough, then sent to a pulmonary specialist. A pulmonary function test confirmed what I already felt—my lung capacity had been reduced.

The smoke from this fire wasn't like a normal brush fire. It wasn't just chaparral—it was thousands of homes, vehicles, plastics, lithium-ion batteries, and synthetic materials burning together. We breathed it for weeks. The cost wasn't abstract. For me, it had become personal.

~~~~~

Inside the department, Battalion Chief Aaron Guggenheim, who oversees the LAFD's Wellness Section, took those risks seriously. He worked closely with medical professionals to track both the immediate and long-term impacts of what firefighters were exposed to during the Palisades deployment.

Chief Guggenheim often pointed out that what we faced here wasn't simply brush smoke—it was "urban conflagration" smoke. That kind of exposure raises questions we won't fully answer for years.

The comparison he and others drew was to 9/11. At Ground Zero, firefighters and first responders worked for weeks in toxic air, often without respiratory protection. Only later did the cancers, lung disease, and cognitive challenges surface. The scale was different, but the lesson was the same: the flames aren't the only danger. Sometimes the air itself is the deadliest part.

Recent research has confirmed that the risks we felt could be deeply real and long-lasting. A newly published study of 42 firefighters who responded to the January 2025 fires found more than 60 significant changes in blood proteins after the deployment—proteins tied to immune response, inflammation, oxidative stress, and even cancer-related pathways. These changes were not minor or temporary: they reflect a physiological shift that, according to the authors, may increase long-term disease risk. In other words, what we breathed—not just smoke, but the chemical fallout from burning neighborhoods and the everyday materials of modern life—didn't simply irritate our lungs. It rewrote parts of our biochemistry, leaving a legacy of exposure that may surface years down the road.

Nick Schuler, a veteran Public Information Officer, was trusted to help shape messaging during California's most destructive wildfires in the past. But even with that experience, this one tested him in new ways. "In my 27 years in the fire service, the Palisades and Eaton Fire was the first time I truly worried about the long-term impact on my own health—because of both what was burning and the extended exposure we faced on the frontlines."

~~~~~

The physical damage was only part of the weight. The mental toll was just as serious.

Trauma for first responders accumulates: fires, rescues that don't succeed, funerals, and exposures you can't see. The hard truth is that more firefighters now die by suicide than in the line of duty. The Palisades Fire added to that burden—long shifts, relentless conditions, and the sight of entire neighborhoods erased in hours. Fatigue, stress, and the emotional weight of what we saw doesn't vanish with containment.

For years, the culture was "suck it up." Don't talk about it. Don't show weakness. But silence has a cost. Slowly, that culture is changing. Departments, unions, and leaders are saying out loud what was once whispered: mental health matters. Asking for help is not failure—it's strength.

Schuler put the devastation in stark terms. "After responding to thousands of fires in my career, the devastation from this one was difficult to witness. Each home lost represented a family and a lifetime of memories forever gone. It's a sobering experience—one you can't fully understand unless you've lived through it."

His words echoed what so many of us felt: that the Palisades Fire was not just another deployment. It left scars—on lungs, on minds, and on hearts—that would take far longer to heal than the land itself.

~~~~~

The most effective support isn't always a program—it's a person. Firefighters checking on each other after a hard shift. Sitting at the kitchen table at 2:00 a.m. and asking, "Are you okay?" That simple question, asked at the right time, can carry more weight than any policy.

During the Palisades deployment, I saw it in small, practical ways. Crews who had worked 36 hours straight still made sure their partners had food and water. Strike team members quietly looked out for each other after walking residents through burned-out neighborhoods. That brotherhood mattered.

Support also came from beyond the fire service. Actors, athletes, and community figures stepped in quietly, wanting to help in any way they could. Jay Leno rolled up to base camp in his vintage fire truck, serving barbecue late into the night. Gary Sinise did the same, without fanfare. Justin Turner and his wife came out to serve food until sundown.

These weren't headline moments, but they mattered. When fatigue weighed heavy, those simple gestures restored morale. They reminded us that the residents of Los Angeles had our back—that the city we served saw us not just as uniforms, but as people.

At the same time, support was being built into the larger system. FEMA recovery centers didn't just help with insurance paperwork and lost vital records—they offered referrals for mental health counseling. The Red Cross went further, proactively reaching out to families to discuss eligibility for financial assistance and emotional support. Even in recovery, behavioral health was finally being treated as part of the disaster response.

Peer support teams, chaplains, counseling services, K9 therapy, resilience training—all are more available now than they were even a decade ago. But tools only work if people use them. The fire service is still learning how to make mental wellbeing part of the job, the same way training and safety are.

~~~~~

The Palisades Fire underscored the weight we carry—but it also highlighted the progress being made. Firefighters who once would have stayed silent are now reaching out. Leaders are modeling vulnerability, and behavior breeds behavior. The definition of brotherhood is shifting—not just working side by side on a hoseline, but standing with each other long after the smoke clears.

That gives me hope. Because if there's one lesson from this fire that applies beyond tactics and training, it's this: resilience isn't just about rebuilding homes. It's about rebuilding people. And that work continues, long after the last ember dies.

From inside an LAFD helicopter, an aircrew captured the Palisades Fire smoke header, bent sharply sideways by powerful winds over the rugged terrain. Credit: LAFD AirOps

A distant view of the Hurst Fire as a powerful column of smoke rises over steep, remote terrain on January 12, 2025. Credit: ALERTCalifornia, UC San Diego

Erik Scott

An Inspector's vehicle swept off Pacific Coast Highway during the February 13 mudflows, illustrating the sudden force of post-fire debris movement. Credit: Justin Michaels, The Weather Channel

LAFD Heavy Rescue lifts the Inspector's vehicle from the cliffside during a complex recovery operation following the February 13 mudflows. Credit: LAFD Erik Scott

On the Pacific Coast Highway, Erik Scott joins an elderly couple in a moment of support as they face the remains of their home.
Credit: Angelica Perez

Erik Scott

Operational Briefing at the Zuma Beach Command Post, where hundreds of firefighters and law-enforcement personnel gathered at first light to coordinate the next operational period.

A sweeping view of the Palisades burn scar at sunset, where entire neighborhoods were reduced to ash in mere hours. From this vantage point above PCH, the scale of destruction becomes unmistakably clear—thousands of structures lost, families displaced, and a community beginning the long road to recovery. Credit: Ben Sarao

Calm Amidst Chaos

Sean Penn and Ann Lee of CORE speak with Captain Erik Scott amid the burned remains of a Palisades neighborhood, coordinating relief efforts in the days after the fire. Credit: Jaya, CORE Response

Erik Scott

A resident walks through the ashes of what was once their home, protected by full hazmat gear against the toxic debris left behind. Recovery here wasn't just emotional—it required real physical protection and courage to confront what remained. Credit: Ben Sarao

At the Getty Villa with Larry Vein, the heart behind Pali Strong. Honored to receive this medal from a man who helped lift an entire community when it mattered most. Credit: Lauren Scott

Erik Scott

Part 3

FROM ASHES TO THE SPOTLIGHT

Chapter 15

INVITATIONS TO HOLLYWOOD'S BIGGEST STAGES

"Who do you want to meet tonight?"

~ *Grae Drake, the Critics' Choice Association*

The Palisades Fire had barely cooled when life took a surreal turn. One week we were walking streets still lined with rubble and skeletal chimneys where neighborhoods once stood, and the next we were holding invitations to Hollywood's brightest stages.

We were invited to the Critics' Choice Awards, the SAG Awards, and eventually the Oscars. Because leadership was still overseeing recovery—and mindful of sensitivities—they didn't attend. Instead, they asked us, the department's public information team, to represent.

Hollywood itself was uncertain. Some questioned whether ceremonies should be canceled out of respect; others believed they should continue as an act of strength. In the end, they chose to move forward, but with moments of acknowledgment for the losses our city had endured. Firefighters became a natural bridge— visible reminders that endurance was real, but so was devastation. Celebrities often remarked that *music and movies were healing*—that art could provide comfort even as the city grieved.

Erik Scott

The first of the major invitations came from the *Critics' Choice Awards*, held on February 7, 2025, at the Barker Hangar in Santa Monica. It wasn't just LAFD. Firefighters, officers, and paramedics from across Southern California were asked to attend—Los Angeles County, Santa Monica, Beverly Hills, Culver City, Long Beach, Ventura County, and even CAL FIRE. LAPD also joined us, along with Red Cross and Habitat for Humanity representatives. It was the definition of a multi-agency showing, a reminder that no one fought the January fires alone.

Everyone arrived in dress uniform. Fifteen members from LAFD joined ten more from neighboring agencies. Even K9 therapy handlers were present, their dogs instantly recognizable, beloved for the comfort they bring on the fireline and warmly welcomed on a red carpet.

Captain Adam Van Gerpen and I oversaw the flow of attending the event so that every department could participate fully and still enjoy the experience. A bus picked us up from Fire Station 59 in West LA, and when we stepped off together in Santa Monica, it felt both surreal and unifying—a brotherhood of agencies forged in the same flames.

We walked the red carpet as a group, posed for photos, and then made our way into the massive hangar. In the lobby, before the show began, I met Grae Drake, a senior producer and board member of the Critics' Choice Association. She immediately put us at ease, calling us her "new besties," and later joked in an email that she had made sure we had pretzels and ice cream rather than drinks—an amusing note she added after I'd mentioned that, glamorous venue or not, we were still there in uniform.

Once the show started, Grae quietly slipped over to our table. She explained that during commercial breaks, it was a free-for-all—those brief windows where you could get up, move around, and strike up conversations before the music signaled everyone back to their seats. She used that time to ask each firefighter, "Who do you want to meet tonight?" and then she made it happen.

For me, that led to an unforgettable introduction to Angelina Jolie. The first thing I told her was, "My wife is your biggest fan." She smiled warmly, and what followed was a genuine, unhurried conversation that lasted the entire break. I commended her humanitarian work, telling her how impressed I was by it. We even talked about our shared love of cars as the film *Gone in 60 Seconds* has long been one of my favorites, and I've always had a soft spot for classic Shelbys.

Apparently, we were talking long enough that the tabloids noticed. The *Daily Mail* ran photos of the exchange under the headline: "Angelina Jolie enjoys chat with LA firefighters at Critics' Choice Awards after missing out on Maria trophy."

Throughout it all, we spoke with mutual respect—two people from very different worlds but sharing a conversation that was heartfelt and sincere. As the music swelled to bring everyone back to their seats, she clasped my hand with both of hers in parting, before we each scattered back to our tables.

Later, Kathy Bates accepted her award for Best Actress in a TV Drama. In her speech, she thanked the Los Angeles Fire Department directly, noting that her producer, Eric Olsen, had lost his home in the Palisades Fire. Sitting there in that room, hearing those words, was powerful—a reminder that our work touched lives far beyond the fireline.

During one commercial break, Host Chelsea Handler joined our table, prepping for the cameras to turn back on. Off-air, she leaned over and shared a few laughs with us. Earlier in the show, she had set the tone perfectly:

"My hope for tonight is to take our time here together and use

Erik Scott

it to remind each other and everyone watching of the resilience and determination that is within all of us when we come together as a community, with a huge debt of gratitude to our honored guests tonight—the firefighters, Red Cross, and Habitat for Humanity volunteers."

When the night ended and the bus rolled back toward West LA, I felt a quiet pride. The event had gone smoothly, every agency had been represented, and—for a few hours—we had been more than first responders. We had been guests of honor in a city that rarely pauses to say thank you.

~~~~~

Just two weeks later, firefighters from across Southern California were invited to the 31st Annual Screen Actors Guild Awards, held on February 23, 2025, at the Shrine Exposition Hall. Eighteen tickets were reserved for first responders, and I was particularly honored to have gotten members from Fire Station 23 to attend the event and be seated at our table. Based in the Pacific Palisades, they had been in the thick of January's battle and truly "fought the fine fight."

From the beginning, we made an extra effort to incorporate members from Stations 23 and 69, since they were housed in the Palisades during the fire, and to involve firefighters who had lost their homes in the blaze. These award shows were not just about recognition—they were about giving space to those who had sacrificed so much and making sure they could experience a well-deserved tactical pause after such a relentless start to the year.

Walking the red carpet together in dress uniform, we posed for a group photo and gave short interviews for the pre-show. From the start, the atmosphere felt different. This wasn't just another awards show—it was one of Hollywood's biggest stages, broadcast live on Netflix, with the full weight of the industry present.

Inside, the tone was humbling. Celebrities approached us with gratitude, telling stories of wildfires near their neighborhoods, sharing how firefighters had helped their families in years past. Some expressed shock at the scale of devastation, asking, "How could this happen?" Inevitably, those conversations turned to the unprecedented wind conditions—how we couldn't stop the fire until the winds themselves finally relented. Those who were in Los Angeles during that week understood; they had felt those winds firsthand and described being "blown away," not literally, but in the sheer force of it all.

For me, the highlight was a full-circle moment with Harrison Ford. I first met him in 2018, when he flew his helicopter to Malibu to record wildfire Public Service Announcements (PSA). You can still hear his voice on the wildfire safety video at lafd.org/wildfire, where he lent his words to our cause.

Now, years later at the SAG Awards, I found myself face-to-face with him again. We reminisced about those days and even talked about the possibility of future collaboration. Sharing that moment with a Hollywood legend was humbling, and it reminded me that wildfires touch everyone in Los Angeles.

The night also gave me an unexpected gift: a serendipitous reunion with Kathy Bates. Just weeks earlier, she had publicly thanked firefighters during her Critics' Choice Awards acceptance speech. Now, when we crossed paths again, it was as if we were old friends. She greeted me with genuine warmth and excitement and offered a heartfelt hug that reminded me compassion travels both ways and sometimes circles back when you least expect it.

As the show unfolded, we found ourselves seated alongside actors from *The Diplomat*. They had just finished bingeing on news coverage of the Palisades Fire, and suddenly, we were swapping

Erik Scott

stories at the same table.

After the ceremony, the atmosphere shifted. The post-awards gala turned into a celebration, and that's when the now-famous dance circle broke out. Mary J. Blige, Meek Mill, and Biggie blasted from the speakers, and several firefighters jumped in. Christopher Scott, the choreographer of *Wicked*, joined the circle, while director Jon M. Chu filmed it all on his phone.

As reporter Jada Yuan later described in the *Washington Post*, the moment captured joy in its purest form—a release after months of tragedy and stress. I was proud of my team. I wasn't dancing; I was on overwatch, the captain making sure everyone was safe and yet had a chance to rightfully soak up their moment.

That night captured something vital. After 28 straight days on the fireline, followed by deployment to the mudslides that came after, this wasn't frivolity, it was a tactical pause, a moment of levity in the middle of a long recovery. The very next morning, we were back to work. But for a few hours, Hollywood gave us the space to breathe, and it meant more than words can capture.

Each event felt bigger than the last. The Critics' Choice Awards was surreal, the SAG Awards even more so. And then came the Oscars—an invitation none of us could have imagined. The scale was historic, and nothing could have prepared us for what happened when we walked onto that stage.

Chapter 16

THE OSCARS

On Oscars night, **Conan O'Brien** set the stage: "Please welcome the real heroes of Los Angeles..."

The Oscars were unlike anything we had experienced. We'd stepped onto red carpets before, but this was the pinnacle—the biggest stage in Hollywood, carrying a weight that went far beyond the show itself.

When the producers first reached out, they emphasized diversity and representation. They wanted firefighters of various ranks and positions from multiple agencies including LAFD, LA County, Pasadena, Long Beach, CAL FIRE, all who responded to the Palisades and Eaton Fires. From those who were selected, three of us were asked to deliver lines: myself, LAFD Pilot Jonith Johnson, and Pasadena Captain Jody Slicker.

Although I served as the lead contact for the Oscars producers, I wasn't navigating it alone. I worked closely with Pasadena Fire Chief Chad Augustin, who struck the perfect balance of professionalism and warmth.

At one point, he called me and said, "Hey, we're thinking of bringing some fire department swag for the producers and pages." He didn't want Pasadena showing up with gifts without us having a chance to do the same. That kind of thoughtfulness impressed me.

We quickly purchased t-shirts, hats, and other fire service memorabilia. When we handed them out to the crew, I told them, "You're now part of the LAFD family."

They hugged us. It was a small thing, but a powerful reminder that gratitude doesn't just flow to the people in the spotlight—it belongs to those working tirelessly behind the curtain too.

~~~~~

Walking into the Dolby Theatre for rehearsal was staggering. I've stood on countless stages and given thousands of interviews, but nothing prepared me for anything of this scale. The seats stretched endlessly back, the balconies stacked high, and giant foam-board headshots of A-list celebrities were scattered throughout. Stand-in actors practiced acceptance speeches as if it were the real night.

There were three rehearsals, held on Thursday, Saturday, and the Sunday morning before the show. Host Conan O'Brien's team handed us the joke scripts to review and test on an audience. Sitting in the auditorium waiting for our turn to rehearse, I flipped through the pages and my eyes widened. I looked over at Chief Augustin; he smirked, and we both knew we were uncomfortable with some of the material.

The jokes were clever and funny, but not all were appropriate for us to deliver while in uniform. It wasn't the right moment to interrupt rehearsals, so we went through them as written, and some even drew big laughs. Afterward, I asked the producer if we could speak with the writers. When we met with the head writer, we thanked them for including us and explained how honored we were to be part of such a major event. At the same time, we made clear that a few of the jokes crossed lines we couldn't cross while representing our departments. We have a code of conduct to uphold, and we hoped they would understand. To our appreciation, they did, and they rewrote the scripts.

On the night of the 97th Academy Awards, layers of security ushered us backstage. It was almost like moving through levels of a tunnel system as we inched closer to the stage. Each holding area brought us closer to showtime. We were guided down narrow corridors, past green rooms, and through dimly lit alleys where you'd occasionally catch a glimpse of an A-list actor or hear a voice you instantly recognized. Eventually, we reached a larger staging room filled with people in headsets watching monitors and reviewing the run-of-show. That's where all of us firefighters gathered.

I suggested we stand in uniformity—left hand over right, not behind our backs or at our sides—to project the same professionalism we bring to an incident. We were split into two groups, one on each side of the stage. As our moment approached, they lined us up just out of sight, the final threshold before stepping into the lights.

When Conan introduced us, the entire room erupted—a thunderous standing ovation that hit us before we ever reached our marks. Walking toward center stage, seeing every person rise to their feet, was overwhelming; the applause didn't taper off—it *built*. I remember dropping my head for a moment, stunned by the sincerity of it, before we steadied ourselves and got ready to deliver our lines.

Conan set the stage: "Please welcome the real heroes of Los Angeles…"

I went first: "Our hearts go out to all those who lost their homes. I'm talking about the producers of *Joker 2*."

The joke carried a little sting. Some people laughed, others didn't, and that contrast was exactly what made it bold. Soon, outlets from *The Washington Post* to the *Daily Mail* were quoting it, calling it "the joke heard around the world."

Jonith Johnson followed with: "To play Bob Dylan, Timothée Chalamet learned how to sing. In fact, his singing was so good he almost lost the part."

And then Captain Jody Slicker delivered the closer: "It's great to be back with Conan. Usually when he calls, it's because he's stuck in a tree."

The laughter and applause rolled. For that moment, firefighters weren't just observers—we were part of the show.

~~~~~

What happened backstage was just as unforgettable. Mick Jagger appeared out of nowhere to greet us. On our way back, Miley Cyrus smiled as we crossed paths. And then, just outside the green room, Adam Sandler stepped out, stopped me, and said: "That was one hell of a delivery."

He grabbed my phone and snapped a selfie with me and another firefighter. I grew up watching his movies, so that kind and spontaneous gesture is etched in my memory forever.

The night didn't end at the Dolby Theatre. We were given tickets to the Governor's Ball, Hollywood's most exclusive after-party. Winners mingled with producers and executives, the energy buzzing in every corner.

For me, though, it felt oddly familiar. Like a community pancake breakfast or a fire station open house—meeting people, answering questions, connecting. The only difference was that this "community" happened to be Hollywood's elite. Same uniform, same approach, just amplified to the highest level.

~~~~~

One of the firefighters who joined us at the various events was Jake Heflin. "It was truly a humbling experience to be on an international stage," Jake reflected. "As firefighters, we don't do what we do for accolades or acknowledgment. We do what we do out of duty." He spoke for all of us when he added, "We are simply representatives of the fire service as a whole... a small snapshot reflecting firefighters and professional staff that rallied to support the community in its time of need."

Then came one of those perfect human moments that cut through the glamour. Before the Oscars, Jake's stepdaughter handed him a homemade autograph book and asked him to get a few signatures. During a break backstage, Selena Gomez passed by. He politely asked if she might sign it, and she graciously did—an act captured on film and shared by *People Magazine*. His stepdaughter saw the photo and burst into tears. "She was so proud," he said. "That little book had its viral moment."

~~~~~

When the glitter faded, what I wanted most was to reconnect with family. I met my wife Lauren at a small pizza joint in Hollywood. We shared a couple of slices, a glass of wine, and tried to wrap our heads around the night.

The standing ovation, the jokes, the Governor's Ball—all of it was surreal. But the truest moment was sitting across from my wife, grounding myself in the reality that no matter how big the stage, it always comes back to family.

Erik Scott

Chapter 17

THE LOS ANGELES PRESS CLUB

"Another major hit to the head could put you in a wheelchair."
~ Treating physicians after the collapse

The Los Angeles Press Club has always held a special place in my heart. In 2025, the organization extended an invitation for me to help hand out awards to Los Angeles's major TV networks for their coverage of the January wildfires. It was a tremendous honor—made even more meaningful because the ceremony was held at the historic Los Angeles Biltmore, the very place where Lauren and I had been married back in 2008.

To make the moment even more full circle, the Biltmore was also where, in 2011, I stood on that same stage with my fellow PSOs Brian Humphrey and Matt Spence to receive First Place for Best Blog from the Los Angeles Press Club, in coordination with the International Association of Fire Fighters (IAFF.) Returning there years later, on June 22, 2025, now handing out the awards that had meant so much to us, felt like life had closed a loop.

That weekend had already been full. Lauren and I had rushed back from Long Beach after attending a three-day religious convention that we look forward to every year. It's always a highlight, a chance to recharge and ground myself in a fast-paced world. From there, we shifted gears, changed into formal attire, and headed straight downtown to the Biltmore.

As we entered, we posed for photos against a backdrop wall filled with sponsor logos and bright lights—just like reporters and honorees do before the show. This time, though, I wasn't standing there with media outlets but standing proudly on the red carpet with my wife.

~~~~~

Somewhere along the way that evening, I was asked a familiar question: "How did you come to be the spokesperson for the Los Angeles Fire Department?"

The truth traces back to a single night—when a roof fell on my head and the trajectory of my entire career shifted in seconds.

I thought back. It was the middle of the night, the station finally settled into that rare stillness where you can actually fall asleep. Then the PA system cracked open the dark: "Structure fire. Eighty-nine's first-in."

Adrenaline erased whatever rest you had. Jump in your boots, pull your turnouts up, and slide on the red suspenders. Now run. The engine bay was already alive—diesel rumbling, overhead doors rising—as we climbed aboard and threw on our headsets. Engine 7 had been busy all day; tonight would be no exception.

I was riding hydrant, responsible for securing the water supply. En route, the report came: an elderly couple possibly trapped inside. That sharpened everything—gear checks, radio discipline, and mental prep for my rookie who had the nozzle.

I turned the dial on my handheld to the tach channel to get more situational awareness and turned up the volume as we rolled toward the address. The glow hit first: a deep orange smear against the sky, a black column rising behind it. That kind of visual confirmation spikes your adrenaline every time—you know you're seconds from heat, chaos, and decisions that matter.

Radio traffic crackled with urgency. The Incident Commander was already talking about exposures—fire threatening to extend into nearby homes. We were assigned to protect the Delta exposure, the house on the right when viewed from the street.

The engineer stayed at the pump panel. My rookie and I grabbed hose off the transverse bed and stretched the line down the right side yard, our captain behind us on the radio. The radiant heat off the main structure was intense. After protecting the exposure, we pushed through the backyard and swung left toward the Charlie side—the rear—preparing to make entry for a secondary search inside.

Conditions were heavy, dark, and loud.

And that's when it happened.

In this profession, you're trained to spot the warning signs of collapse—how long the fire has been burning, the thickness of the wood, sagging rooflines, spongy floors, cracking beams. But sometimes, even with all that training, there are failures you cannot predict.

That night, one of them found me.

Without warning, a massive crushing weight slammed down on the top of my helmet. The impact drove me forward to the ground, my body folding in half until my head was jammed between my knees. All the weight pressed onto my air bottle, tacoing me in half and leaving me trapped beneath the burning debris. I remember it like it was yesterday.

The adrenaline masked the pain, but the reality was clear: I was pinned hard! I tried pressing upward with all my might, but nothing. Reverting to my training, I yelled out: "Firefighter

Erik Scott

trapped!" Shortly thereafter, I vigorously tried rolling sideways but couldn't. I took a deep breath and tried to lift my head back to see anything. I couldn't; it was pitch black. I called out again: "Firefighter trapped!" Then strove to grab at anything in front of me to pull myself forward—nothing.

I had full confidence in the seasoned firefighters around me and knew I would be found. My captain and rookie were close, and other crews were working inside. Still, minutes tend to feel like hours when you're pinned in a fire and can't move.

I tried everything—pressing upward, trying to roll, attempting to crawl forward—but the weight wouldn't budge, and no one could hear me. So I went for the one tool I still had: my radio. Muscle memory took over in the hot darkness. My radio is always in the same left pocket, the mic in the upper right. But bent in half and compressed like that, my arms had almost no reach. They were like little T-rex arms—short, stiff, and compromised in that position.

I shouted, "Firefighter trapped!" for a third time.

My next thought was the emergency trigger. If I could hit that button, it would sound the distinct high–low tone on the fireground tac channel, and our 911 dispatch center would know exactly who it was from my radio designation. I groped for it, but the dexterity just wasn't there. I could find the area, but not the button, so I used my left hand to take off the glove on my right hand so I could reach across my chest to the radio in my left pocket. It was still nearly impossible to reach, and exposing my bare hand to the heat wasn't worth the risk of a burn. I slid the glove back on, controlled my breathing, and stayed calm.

Through the roar of water streams, chainsaws, and engines, I finally heard voices. What I didn't know at that moment was that my captain had also been struck in the partial roof collapse. The impact knocked him to the ground, leaving half of his body covered in debris. When crews forced their way toward our position, they saw him first and rushed to free him.

Then a beam of light cut through the darkness. Firefighters had found me. It took three or four of them to lift enough debris for me to crawl forward, toward the light.

"You okay! You okay, man?" they asked.

"Yeah," I insisted, already trying to painfully push my way back into the house, determined to finish the assignment. My bell had been rung hard, though, and my crew wisely held me back. They stripped off my gear piece by piece—helmet, bottle, axe, coat—then got their arms under me, shouldering my weight and guiding me carefully through the collapse zone and out the side yard.

The cool air hit me as we stepped outside. Somewhere behind us, a voice came over the radio announcing that I'd been located. My crew walked me toward the waiting gurney in front of the house.

Out front, the medic team was already tending to a patient— an elderly woman in a white nightgown, gray hair matted with smoke. As they worked, they began readying a second gurney nearby—this one for one of their own.

I've been an EMT and Paramedic since 2002, but for the first time, I was in the back of a rescue ambulance—not as a medic, but as a patient.

The collapse left me with injuries from occipital to lumbar—a compressed spine that doctors years later described as "permanent and stationary", as good as it was going to get. Their warning was blunt: another major hit to the head could put me in a wheelchair. My right retina still leaks to this day. Physical therapy became routine.

I hadn't planned to be a spokesperson. My goal had been to

Erik Scott

become an Apparatus Operator—the firefighter who drives the ladder truck. I was tall, strong, and years earlier had been named Top Overall Recruit and earned the Golden Rung for ladder operations. AO felt like the natural path.

But that night changed everything. I spent a full year off the line, temporarily totally disabled (TTD), attending what ultimately became hundreds of rehabilitation appointments. When I finally returned, it was on a light-duty assignment—and that's when I was introduced to the PIO world, a job I hadn't even known existed. It wasn't the career I'd envisioned, but it was the hand I was dealt, and I embraced it. I was selected to serve as a Public Service Officer and, years later, promoted to Captain I.

When I was asked to come to headquarters to be the lead spokesperson, I said I was humbled by the offer but passed—I wanted to diversify. Two weeks later, I was "voluntold," and since then have been honored to highlight the great work our firefighters perform. A couple of years later, I was promoted to Captain II, stayed in the role, and the rest is history.

The roof collapse in North Hollywood reshaped my future. It forced me into a different lane of service—one that ultimately placed me in position to be the face and voice of the Los Angeles Fire Department during the Palisades Fire.

Flashback ends. Story told. Now back to matters at hand…

~~~~~

Inside the Biltmore, my wife and I mingled in the silent auction area for a brief meet-and-greet. But I couldn't help myself—I've always been one to overprepare. So while others enjoyed the reception, I slipped backstage to talk with the producers and the audio-visual team. I wanted to know the flow of the show: where we would stand, how the awards would be handed off, how we could ensure everyone fit on stage without awkwardness. That's the way I approach nearly every assignment—I'd rather over-prepare than under-prepare, rather be overdressed than under-dressed, and rather be early than merely on time. Prepare, adjust, execute.

When the time came, Lauren and I found our assigned seats at a large round table near the front, stage right. To my delight, we were seated with Diana Ljungaeus, the Executive Director of the Press Club. It gave me an opportunity to have a thoughtful conversation about the evening's program and the meaning behind recognizing journalism in such a turbulent year.

Lauren handed me the printed program, and inside was a short bio that caught me off guard. It reminded me of all the steps and stages I'd walked through to arrive here:

*"**Captain Erik Scott** is a Fire Captain II / Paramedic and the Public Information Officer (PIO) for The Los Angeles Fire Department. With nearly 25 years of experience—including prior service with the City of Fillmore—he is known for his leadership, remaining calm amidst chaos, and dedication to public service.*

Captain Scott began his LAFD career as the Top Overall Recruit and holds an Associate of Science in Emergency Medical Services and a Bachelor of Science in Emergency Services Management, graduating with a 4.0 GPA. He has been recognized as Firefighter of the Month, served as a UCLA paramedic instructor, trained as a Terrorism Liaison Officer, and is a graduate of the West Point LAFD Leadership Academy.

As LAFD's spokesperson, he has conducted thousands of media interviews across local, national, and international outlets. He was the trusted voice during the Palisades Fire and is frequently deployed statewide as a Type 1 PIO during major

wildfires. A frequent keynote speaker, Captain Scott is also deep-
ly committed to youth mentorship and community service."

Reading that while sitting next to my wife at the very hotel where we had exchanged vows seventeen years earlier— it was humbling.

~~~~~

Before I stepped into the lights, the organizers played a moving fire montage—a several-minute recap of the intense, unrelenting media coverage from the Palisades Fire. Walls of flame, helicopters banking through smoke, exhausted crews, evacuees clutching pets, live shots from the beach—all of it still raw. You could feel the room shift. Conversations quieted. People leaned forward. Eyes watered. The images hit with the same force they had months earlier, and emotion rippled across the ballroom.

As the last frame faded, the house lights dimmed slightly, and the emcee stepped to the microphone. That's when Robert Kovacik offered an introduction I didn't expect—kind, generous, and far more personal than anything I'd prepared for. He spoke about the fire, about the chaos, and about the need for a steady voice. Then he said that during those critical days, I had become "the one voice we all turned to and trusted."

Hearing that—from Robert, of all people—felt like the moment everything connected: the fire, the work, the partnership between the press and the department, the countless briefings, the nonstop interviews, the weight of those long days. And then, with the audience still silent from the video and his words hanging in the air, I walked onto the stage. The room rose in a standing ovation—before I even set foot on stage. It was only the second standing ovation of my life.

Calm Amidst Chaos

The first was at the Oscars, for all firefighters and first re-sponders. This time it was personal. It felt undeserved—and deep-ly humbling—born of fifteen years as a spokesperson, grinding to build trust with the public and the press. When Robert Kovacik and Pat Harvey called me forward, I hadn't been asked to prepare remarks about them. My role was simple: thank the reporters in at-tendance. But at that moment, I had to acknowledge the two icons standing beside me. I turned first to Pat.

"Pat Harvey—a true trailblazer who has defined prime-time anchoring. The longest-running anchor in prime time at one station in Los Angeles. For her 20th anniversary, the City and County of Los Angeles declared October 30, 2009, Pat Harvey Day. I'm hum-bled to be in your presence."

As the words left my mouth, I caught her reaction—subtle but unmistakably sincere. Pat tilted her head, a warm smile break-ing through as she placed both hands over her chest and mouthed, "thank you." It was a small gesture, but it carried a depth of grati-tude and humility that stood out even in a room filled with bright lights and television legends.

Then I turned to Robert: "Robert Kovacik—not only led this Press Club with distinction but continues to set the standard for journalistic integrity. He has not only won the trust and respect of his audience, but he has also won their hearts with solid reporting." (More applause filled the room.)

Then I addressed the room—the reporters and photojournal-ists I've stood beside for years on firelines and in neighborhoods, people I consider colleagues.

"When January's fires struck, it wasn't just firefight-ers who responded—it was all of you. You weren't just observers; you were part of the emergency response. Our local reporters worked around the clock to keep the public

Erik Scott

informed. You stood by our side, saw the same flames, smelled the same smoke. And because of your compassion, residents told you their stories. They entrusted you with information. You gave them hope and resilience.

Information is a commodity. When we share it—timely, accurate, and consistent—we earn credibility, and credibility saves lives.

The partnership between public safety and the press is vital. It's something we value and respect. On behalf of the LAFD, thank you for the role you played in those critical hours—and for the work you do every day. Stay safe. Stay sharp."

As the applause finally settled and the lights eased back, I took my seat beside Lauren and felt something rare in this line of work: stillness. For a moment, the storms, the flames, the interviews, and the long nights all converged into one truth — none of us do this alone. Not firefighters. Not journalists. Not the communities we serve.

The Los Angeles Press Club was celebrating a year of powerful journalism, public service, and the partnership that carries communities through their hardest moments, and I was humbled to play even a small role in it.

As my wife and I walked out of the Biltmore ballroom hand in hand, I was reminded that resilience doesn't come only from surviving disaster— it comes from the people who stand with you through it.

The Palisades Fire descends toward Malibu under hurricane-force winds, casting an orange glow across the coastline. Credit: CALFire

Looking through a scorched window frame at the charred landscape beyond—trees stripped bare and homes reduced to ash.
Credit: Harry Garvin

Erik Scott

A firefighter advances a hose line through a narrow residential corridor as wind-driven flames and embers press against fences and structures during the Palisades Fire—an intimate, high-risk fight where inches matter and conditions change by the second.

Actor Harrison Ford greets Erik Scott during a 2018 interaction, a moment that reflected his longstanding support for first responders.

MORE STORIES

Angelina Jolie enjoys chat with LA firefighters at Critics Choice Awards after missing out on Maria trophy

By CARLY JOHNSON FOR DAILYMAIL.COM and BRIAN MARKS FOR DAILYMAIL.COM

05:16 08 Feb 2025, updated 06:17 08 Feb 2025

Angelina Jolie and Erik Scott smiling while talking
at Critics Choice Awards. Credit: Daily Mail

Calm Amidst Chaos

LBFD Chief Heflin shares a special Oscars moment as actress Selena Gomez pauses to sign an autograph book for his stepdaughter, a brief and personal exchange amid the night's ceremony and pageantry.

Erik Scott

Selena Gomez leaves the Oscars early but makes a firefighter's night

Selena Gomez and fiancé Benny Blanco made an early exit, leaving the Dolby during the in-memoriam tribute. But on the way out the door, Gomez made the day of Los Angeles firefighter Jake Heflin by signing the adorable autograph book handmade by the emergency responder's 9-year-old stepdaughter. Heflin flagged down Gomez, who held up foot traffic to sign the important paper.

"She told me I had to get Ariana Grande or Selena Gomez," Heflin told USA TODAY of his stepdaughter. Mission accomplished.

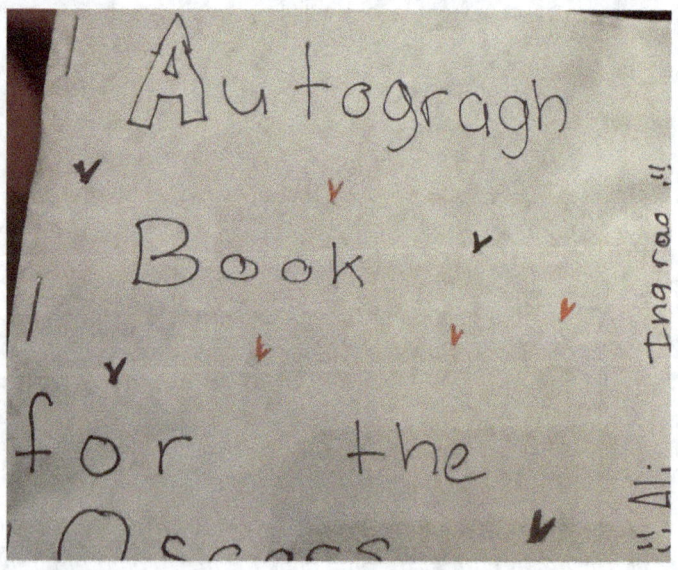

News profile highlighting Jake Heflin's moment at the Oscars, where Selena Gomez paused to sign his 9-year-old stepdaughter's handmade autograph book—a small act of kindness on a very big night.
Credit: USA Today

Backstage at the Oscars, firefighters stand with a show producer they had worked closely with throughout the night—a gracious and supportive partner behind the scenes.

Erik Scott

Lauren and Erik Scott grab a selfie after slipping out for a late slice of pizza in Hollywood—finally catching their breath and reconnecting after the whirlwind of Oscars night.

*At the 67th Los Angeles Press Club Awards, Erik's remarks drew
an emotional response from anchor Pat Harvey, while NBC's Robert
Kovacik looked on with a proud smile—a moment that captured
the deep bond between journalists and the first responders they cover.*

Erik Scott

Part 4

CLOSURE, LESSONS,
LEADERSHIP, REFLECTIONS

Chapter 18

CAUSE AND CLOSURE

"A former Pacific Palisades resident now living in Florida has been arrested on a federal criminal complaint charging him with maliciously starting what eventually became the Palisades Fire of January 2025."

~ *U.S. Department of Justice, Oct. 8, 2025*

F or months, one question hung in the air like smoke that refused to lift: How did it start?

Residents wanted to understand what had taken their homes, their sense of safety, and, tragically for some, their loved ones. Firefighters wanted answers too—not out of blame, but for lessons learned. We live, work, and play in L.A. We left blood, sweat, and tears on that hillside for weeks, and after the flames died down and the smoke cleared, we were often the shoulders people cried on. We cared. We wanted answers, too. Cause determination isn't about punishment; it's about prevention, clarity, and truth.

The answer arrived on a clear and bright morning, with a hint of fall in the air— October 8, 2025—nine months after that wall of flame had torn through the bluffs and canyons of Pacific Palisades.

I was at LAFD Headquarters when I was summoned to the Fire Chief's Conference Room. We knew this day would come—

Erik Scott

and it finally had. Inside, a handful of senior staff were already gathered, the mood measured and serious. Word had just come down from the U.S. Department of Justice confirming what many had feared: the fire that would later turn deadly had been intentionally set.

As of October 8, 2025, the U.S. Attorney's Office for the Central District of California announced the arrest of a suspect in a federal criminal complaint. The DOJ stated:

"A former Pacific Palisades resident now living in Florida has been arrested on a federal criminal complaint charging him with maliciously starting what eventually became the Palisades Fire of January 2025, one of the most destructive wildfires in Los Angeles history.

Jonathan Rinderknecht, 29, a.k.a. "Jonathan Rinder," and "Jon Rinder," of Melbourne, Florida, is charged with destruction of property by means of fire."

~~~~~

Back at headquarters, our conference room became a kind of nerve center, similar to an Incident Command Post in the early hours of a major fire—focused, fast-moving, and driven by purpose. We talked strategy—what to say, what not to speculate on, and how to balance transparency with accuracy. Within minutes, media requests began to flood in. Phones buzzed. Emails stacked up. We began tracking the onslaught of inquiries—TV, radio, print, English and Spanish language outlets all wanting the same thing: confirmation, quotes, context. We divided tasks, drafted statements, coordinated approvals, and scheduled what interviews we could.

The tone in the building was different that day. We've handled countless media surges before, but this one carried a different kind of gravity. Twelve people had tragically lost their lives, and billions of dollars in damage had reshaped the coastline. It wasn't just about information—it was about closure.

In addition, the DOJ report mentioned:

"Law enforcement determined—using witness statements, video surveillance, cellphone data, and analysis of fire dynamics and patterns at the scene, among other things – that Rinderknecht maliciously set the Lachman Fire just after midnight on January 1 on land owned by the Mountains Recreation and Conservation Authority (MRCA), an organization that received federal funding. A week later, the same fire—then known as the Palisades Fire – burned federal property.

On the evening of December 31, 2024, Rinderknecht was working as an Uber driver. Two passengers that he drove on separate trips between 10:15 p.m. and 11:15 p.m. that night later told law enforcement they remembered that Rinderknecht appeared agitated and angry.

After dropping off a passenger in Pacific Palisades, Rinderknecht – who once lived in that neighborhood – drove towards Skull Rock Trailhead, parked his car, attempted to contact a former friend, and walked up the trail. He then used his iPhone to take videos at a nearby hilltop area and listened to a rap song – to which he had listened repeatedly in previous days – whose music video included things being lit on fire.

At 12:12 a.m. on January 1, 2025, environmental sensing platforms indicated the Lachman Fire had begun. During the next five minutes, Rinderknecht called 911 several times, but didn't get through because his iPhone was out of cellphone range. When he finally connected with 911, he was at the bottom of the hiking trail and reported the fire. By that point, a nearby resident already had reported the fire to authorities.

Erik Scott

Rinderknecht then fled in his car, passing fire engines driving in the opposite direction. He then turned around and followed the fire engines to the scene, driving at a high rate of speed. Rinderknecht walked up the same trail from earlier that night to watch the fire and the firefighters. At approximately 1:02 a.m., he used his iPhone to take more videos of the scene.

During an interview with law enforcement on January 24, 2025, Rinderknecht lied about where he was when he first saw the Lachman Fire. He claimed he was near the bottom of a hiking trail when he first saw the fire and called 911, but geolocation data from his iPhone carrier showed that he was standing in a clearing 30 feet from the fire as it rapidly grew"...

"If convicted, Rinderknecht would face a mandatory minimum sentence of five years in federal prison and a statutory maximum sentence of 20 years in federal prison.

ATF is investigating this matter, with substantial assistance from the Los Angeles Police Department and the United States Forest Service."

The announcement included:

"A complaint contains allegations that a defendant has committed a crime. Every defendant is presumed to be innocent until and unless proven guilty beyond a reasonable doubt in court."

The LAFD then released the following quote:

"Today, the U.S. Department of Justice announced the arrest of a suspect in connection with January's Palisades Fire. This action was deliberate, intended to cause devastating harm to the City of Los Angeles. This arrest is a critical step toward ensuring accountability, justice, and healing for our city.

We are forever grateful to our frontline responders, law enforcement partners, and the people of Los Angeles for their vigilance and support for one another during this incredibly challenging year. Although the flames have been extinguished, the impact of these fires will linger for years to come. Our hearts are with the families and neighborhoods who faced tremendous loss.

The Los Angeles City Fire Department remains committed to protecting our city and standing with our communities as they rebuild and heal. As we enter yet another fire season, we ask all Angelenos to stay alert and report any suspicious activity."

This was a heavy blow to the Palisades community. However, one question remained. How did the January 1 Lachman Fire lead to the January 7 Palisades Fire?

The DOJ report also stated:

"According to an affidavit filed with the complaint, law enforcement determined that the Palisades Fire was a "holdover" fire – a continuation of the Lachman Fire that began early in the morning on New Year's Day 2025. Although firefighters quickly suppressed the Lachman Fire, unbeknownst to anyone the fire continued to smolder and burn underground within the root structure of dense vegetation.

On January 7, heavy winds caused the underground fire to surface and spread above ground in what became known as the Palisades Fire, which caused widespread damage in the Pacific Palisades neighborhood of Los Angeles."

On October 9, 2025, LAFD released the Holdover Fires Fact Sheet, which explained:

"A holdover fire is a deep-rooted smoldering fire that remains dormant or smoldering—without visible flames or spread—for some time after its initial ignition. It can remain undetected or only partially suppressed before re-igniting or flaring up again under favorable conditions. In wildland and forest fire contexts, this often occurs when surface flames die out but smoldering combustion continues deep underground. Once conditions warm, dry, or oxygen becomes available, the smoldering fire may reignite surface fuels, and the fire "returns.""

In chaparral ecosystems, deep, woody root systems can retain heat below the surface after a fire, effectively acting as concealed fuel that may continue to smolder.

"Chaparral species such as manzanita, chamise, ceanothus, and scrub oak have large, lignified root systems that reach deep into the soil to access groundwater— sometimes as far as 15 to 25 feet below the surface. After a surface fire, these roots can continue smoldering underground long after the visible flames are extinguished. Because chaparral roots are woody and resinous, they burn slowly and retain heat for long durations. This slow, oxygen-limited combustion can move through the soil and re-emerge days or even weeks later when the surface dries and winds increase."

Detection is extremely difficult in these conditions.

"Holdover fires in chaparral are extremely difficult to detect using traditional infrared or aerial imaging. In these ecosystems, smoldering can occur deep below the surface—often well beyond the detection range of thermal sensors.

Thermal imaging cameras detect infrared radiation (in the 8–14 µm range) emitted from surface heat, not from subsurface combustion. For heat to be detected, it must conduct through the soil and radiate outward. In dry, mineral-rich, or ash-covered soils—which act as natural insulators—only the upper inch or two may show measurable temperature differences, making deeper heat pockets virtually invisible to detection equipment."

Challenging terrain further complicates suppression efforts.

"Chaparral grows in steep, rugged topography — canyons, ridges, and inaccessible slopes—where digging or trenching to expose smoldering roots is nearly impossible. Ground crews must rely on indirect suppression methods, such as cold trailing or mop-up using hand tools and water drops. However, with root systems running many feet deep, it is nearly impossible to fully extinguish all underground heat pockets."

Wind and drying conditions significantly increase the likelihood of reignition.

"When surface conditions dry out, and strong winds return, latent heat from smoldering roots can reignite fine surface fuels. This is particularly dangerous in chaparral because fuels are continuous and volatile, allowing a single flare-up to spread rapidly upslope. Reignitions can occur days or even weeks after containment."

Similar holdover activity has been documented across Southern California.

"In areas like the Angeles National Forest and the Santa Monica Mountains, post-incident analyses have found that small flare-ups days later often trace back to root-based smoldering in manzanita or chamise stands. These "sleeper fires" can appear 10 to 20 days after initial containment, especially following wind events or extreme drying."

In conclusion:

"Holdover fires are deep-rooted, smoldering fires that can remain undetectable for days or weeks, particularly in chaparral with extensive woody root systems. On January 7, an unprecedented wind event far exceeding typical Santa Ana conditions contributed to the rapid spread and reactivation of a holdover fire, even after aggressive, fully executed suppression efforts. This fire highlights the unpredictable nature of holdover fires despite the department's thorough and timely response. The Los Angeles City Fire Department remains committed to rapid detection, containment, and public safety, recognizing that holdover fires are an inherent risk of managing wildland fire in Southern California."

Erik Scott

~~~~~

After the DOJ announcement broke, the LAFD could release its 78-page After-Action Review Report—an exhaustive study of those first 36 hours. It was both an autopsy and a roadmap for reform. The report cataloged successes and shortcomings with transparency: resource shortages, communication gaps, grounded aircraft, and the strain of managing multiple simultaneous wind-driven fires.

But it also documented the extraordinary.

Crews who hiked into flame-scorched streets to check for residents who hadn't evacuated—one firefighter finding an elderly man asleep under blankets, saving his life. Companies that used pool water when demand exceeded supply. The dozer line that preserved Fire Station 23.

The report wasn't about blame—it was about learning. It highlighted the value of long-standing partnerships, pre-fire coordination with surrounding agencies, and the rapid regional response that unified the city under a single command within hours. It also identified areas for improvement: earlier recalls, stronger communications infrastructure, more qualified overhead personnel, better integration with law enforcement during evacuations, and expanded public-warning systems.

Many of those reforms were already in motion by the time the ink dried. The department overhauled its recall process, added Starlink redundancy, integrated drone mapping with NOVA software for real-time hotspot detection, and strengthened partnerships with MySafe:LA to expand wildfire-preparedness outreach. Members trained on alternative water sourcing and conducted expanded annual evacuation drills using live data.

Those weren't symbolic changes. They were structural—born directly from experience and loss.

~~~~~

For me, that October day never really paused. It was a blur of statements, interviews, approvals, and media coordination that ran straight through the evening. There wasn't time for reflection—only response. Every answer generated new questions, and I knew the public records requests and follow-ups would stretch for months. When someone asked whether the arrest brought closure, I wanted to believe it did, but the truth was more complicated.

In many ways, the entire Palisades Fire experience had unfolded in peaks and valleys—intense surges followed by brief lulls. The first 72 hours were relentless, a blur of wind, flame, and information that felt impossible to keep up with until we found our battle rhythm. Then came steadier days, the gradual demobilization, and a short pause to breathe—only for the rains to arrive, bringing debris flows and another round of emergency messaging for the mudslides.

Months later, the pace spiked again during awards season, honoring the brave firefighters and first responders who served. As things began to level out, the DOJ announcement and the After-Action Review reignited public attention. Questions multiplied. Through every phase, our small public information team did what we always do—prioritize, triage, stay professional, and maintain composure under pressure. Still, it all felt small in comparison.

Closure, in our world, rarely comes clean. It arrives in pieces—one headline, one report, one slow realization that the city endured. Our hearts went out to all those who lost so much.

I remember driving out of Headquarters that night after the final interview, the sky over downtown streaked with the same pastel glow it had the evening the Palisades Fire finally went cold.

Erik Scott

There are four phases of emergency management: mitigation, preparedness, response, and the long road to recovery. We often remind one another that an incident isn't over when the flames go out. The Palisades Fire proved that.

And as I stood beneath that glowing October sky, I realized something that's stayed: true steadiness isn't the absence of chaos—it's how we move through it, as a team, one clear decision at a time.

Chapter 19

THE AFTER-ACTION REVIEW

"LAFD needs to be fully funded and fully staffed. Period."

~ Councilwoman Traci Parks

When the Los Angeles Fire Department's After-Action Review Report was scheduled before the Board of Fire Commissioners on October 21, 2025, the room was already tense. The Palisades Fire report had drawn headlines and questions about communication, coordination, and resources.

When the floor opened for comments, the tone in the room shifted. The tension of the report gave way to lived experience—firefighters, union leaders, and city representatives speaking candidly about the conditions exposed by the Palisades Fire. As documented in that Fire Commission meeting, these remarks and excerpts were made during public comment and are part of the public record.

Dave Riles, a Fire Captain and UFLAC Director, spoke first. His delivery was steady but firm.

"UFLAC supports the Fire Chief's request for $200 million in additional funding for the LAFD," he said. "This should be the bare minimum of what we're requesting. Included in that request are the restoration of 42 of the critical Emergency Incident Technicians (EIT) positions, additional staffing for Fast Response Vehicles and Advanced Provider Response Unit (APRU), an additional hand crew, and more funding for fleet replacement."

He warned that the department could not sustain further cuts. "There's no possible way the LAFD can absorb any further reductions," he said.

"Let's fight back against any possible cuts and demand the restoration of the EITs and all the items proposed by the Fire Chief for the next fiscal year."

Next came Doug Coates, UFLAC's First Vice President. His remarks were detailed and direct.

"The After-Action Report once again demonstrated that the LAFD is lacking the personnel and equipment to properly respond to the Palisades Fire," he said. "Our department is half the size it should be on a regular day in LA—but much less on January 7."

He pointed to specifics. "In 2017, due to staffing shortages and financial constraints, Red Flag Warnings were changed from 'shall staff' to 'consider to staff.' It's terrible that staffing and deployment decisions were made based on budget concerns—that's been the case for years."

He continued, "On January 7, 40 engines were broken and unavailable due to mechanical issues, and that's because of the loss of civilian mechanics. Which we've been talking about for years... With more bodies, more rigs, and a better water supply, we could— and I repeat, we could—have saved more homes."

Rich Ramirez, UFLAC's Second Vice President, stepped up next and reiterated the point. "The LAFD is half the size it should be," he said.

He referenced the independent *LAFD Standards of Cover* report that analyzed the department's emergency response capabilities. "That report shows we need 62 new fire stations and 4,000 [additional] firefighters...Our firefighters and paramedics are doing more with less, every budget cut put residents at risk." Ramirez said.

He continued, "That's why UFLAC is moving forward with a ballot measure to create a permanent, $324 million revenue stream for the Fire Department. We're done fighting over crumbs each year—it's time to rebuild the LAFD."

Councilwoman Traci Park spoke last, her remarks bridging advocacy and accountability. The Palisades Fire had occurred within her own council district, directly affecting the communities she represents. For Park, this wasn't an abstract policy discussion—it was a crisis that struck at the heart of her constituency.

"Just ten months ago, I joined you all to talk about the dire need for investment in our Fire Department," she said. "Eight months ago, I returned in the wake of the Palisades Fire to emphasize that funding public safety needed to be the North Star of the current year's budget process. And what happened during this year's budget process, just a few months after the worst fire in the history of Los Angeles? What did the council do to the LAFD budget? They cut 42 critical Emergency Incident Technician firefighter positions. The people who coordinate the resources in large-scale emergencies, and who are the eyes and ears on the ground during Mayday situations. That's what they cut."

She continued, "I'm here today as a witness to the effects of decades of underinvestment. I'm here today as the voice of the thousands of families whose lives were completely upended and forever changed by the Palisades Fire. And I'm here today to speak for the twelve individuals who lost their lives on January 7."

Her tone sharpened as she underscored the systemic issue. "Palisades wasn't just another wildfire, it was the moment the curtain got yanked back on a hard truth we've been dodging for decades. Los Angeles is trying to protect a modern mega-city with a Fire Department staffed, equipped, and funded for the needs of a

Erik Scott

city at least a generation ago."

She expressed concerns listed in the After-Action Review and said that "The LAFD needs to be fully funded and fully staffed. Period." She continued, "To our firefighters, you were heroic in the Palisades, you are heroic everyday. This isn't about your courage, it's about whether the system backing you up is as brave as you are…"

She concluded with a challenge, "If we keep underinvesting in safety, we're going to keep overpaying in loss: homes, business-es, memories, lives. It's a bad bargain, and Angelenos are done pay-ing for it…"

From where I was standing in the back of the room, I could feel the temperature shift. The words weren't attacks; they were appeals. They spoke about readiness, safety, and the shared expec-tation that the city must be equipped to protect its people.

Our team had prepared for this moment carefully. We con-vened beforehand to align messaging, draft remarks, and anticipate the toughest questions from commissioners and the press. I asked Captain Adam VanGerpen to assist with post-meeting inquiries. The tension in the room that morning was unmistakable—thick enough to cut with a knife.

The Interim Fire Chief opened by acknowledging the extraor-dinary bravery of firefighters, first responders, and partner agen-cies, expressing gratitude to those who stood with Los Angeles during its most challenging days. Though he was not at the depart-ment during the Palisades Fire, he emphasized that the After-Ac-tion Review represented an honest accounting and a commitment to improvement. Then he introduced Chief Deputy Joseph Everett, who served as the Incident Commander during the Palisades Fire.

Chief Everett had sat quietly through the meeting, his posture composed, listening as those concerns echoed the same operational challenges he and his team had faced on January 7. When he stepped to the podium in full dress uniform, he identified himself for the record and began delivering the department's findings.

He opened with a clear explanation of how the review was conducted:

"This report was an extensive and comprehensive effort led by members of our department's leadership team. They conducted nearly 100 interviews with company members, support personnel, and officers, analyzed radio communications, photographs, eyewitness accounts, to ensure we had a complete and accurate picture of what occurred and what we learned. Understand this report is not just an administrative exercise. It's a roadmap. It captures both our successes and our areas for improvement. It's the foundation of how we move forward as a department and a city."

He then spoke personally about the impact of the fire:

"For me, personally, this fire hits home. My family has lived and served in the Palisades and Malibu area literally since 1937. I've had a family member as part of the LAFD since that time, continuous service. I continue to live and work in that area. I've seen the first-hand impact the Palisades Fire had on our community. I understand the lives lost, the homes lost, the families displaced, and also the lingering trauma throughout the neighborhoods that I currently live in. My family was evacuated during that fire—during the entire time while I served as the Incident Commander. Understand this is not just another incident. It was a community tragedy, and it will remain part of our city's collective memory for years to come."

Everett described the conditions under which the fire began:

"The Palisades Fire began during extraordinary and historic weather conditions in early 2025. The National Weather Service issued a Particularly Dangerous Situation, also known as a PDS warning—one of the rarest alerts possible. At that time, we faced hurricane-force winds at times exceeding 100 miles an hour, low humidity, prolonged drought conditions that left the brush tinder-dry. The fire ignited in steep, heavily vegetated terrain and a combination of canyons filled with chaparral. This accelerated the spread of the fire and also made access extremely difficult for our firefighters."

He noted that multiple incidents were occurring at the same time:

"Simultaneously, other fires were burning in the region. There was the Sunset Fire, there was the Hearst Fire, and there was the Eaton Fire. This stretched our local resources to their limits. Our aircraft were grounded at times due to sustained winds. Staffing was stretched thin, and communication infrastructure was impacted, leading to our problems in the coordination of communications in certain areas. Despite these conditions, the department mobilized immediately. Crews were on the ground within minutes. Aerial operations began in less than 10 minutes."

He then summarized the first 36 hours of operations:

"Over the first 36 hours we had more than 1,200 firefighters, 350 apparatus, multiple air assets relentlessly working to protect lives and property. Our firefighters performed with extraordinary courage and professionalism under some of the most extreme, severe conditions this city has ever witnessed. More than 30,000 residents were safely evacuated, including thousands of seniors and vulnerable populations. Dozens of homes were saved through aggressive structure defense, creative use of water sources when hydrants failed or pressures dropped. Injuries were at a minimal. I consider that a reflection of our training, situational awareness, and the strict adherence to policy for our members on the ground."

Everett highlighted the multi-agency coordination involved:

"A unified command was established quickly and integrated LAFD, LAPD, Los Angeles County Fire, CAL FIRE, federal agencies including the Coast Guard. This was one of the most complex multi-agency fire operations Los Angeles has seen in years, and it demonstrated the strength of collaboration and coordination among our state, local, and federal agencies. Our use of real-time tracking, GIS mapping, night-flying operations gave us critical situational awareness and helped slow the fire's advancement despite this catastrophic weather."

He addressed the areas identified for improvement:

"As with any incident, we had challenges. The review identifies several key areas for improvement. I'll give you some examples. Communications: several zones experienced radio and network outages, creating temporary gaps in situational awareness and delaying some evacuation messages. Staffing and fatigue: extended overtime periods for the firefighters on the ground and prior to the incident impacted readiness and sustainability. Equipment readiness: some reserve apparatus required maintenance or lacked full brush configuration capability. Coordination and clarity early in the response: overlapping assignments highlighted the need for clear role designations and faster interagency coordination. Understand that we view these not as failures, but as lessons, and we've already implemented major improvements to address each one."

Everett then outlined some of the changes implemented since the fire:

"Since January, the department has taken decisive steps to strengthen operational readiness and organizational resilience. Red Flag mobilization policy: during Red Flag Warnings, all staff and apparatus are now recalled immediately—no delays, no exceptions. Water infrastructure coordination: weekly collaboration between our Fire Marshal and the Los Angeles Department of Wa-

Erik Scott

ter and Power ensures that water pressure, hydrant readiness, and infrastructure status are continually monitored. Training and preparedness: enhanced weather tracking and forecasting tools, improved public warning systems, and evacuation drills tailored to the specific communities. Every firefighter now has defined roles and responsibilities in large-scale brush responses to eliminate ambiguity. Communications and connectivity: deployment of Starlink satellite systems for backup communications when cell or radio are disrupted; expansion of redundant radio repeaters in key wildland-interface areas. Operational readiness: a revised pre-deployment model—resources are now moved into position proactively when fire weather is forecasted. Tactical meetings occur prior to the fire, before ignition events, ensuring immediate response and coordination. Community outreach: we partner with organizations such as MySafe:LA to enhance public education, evacuation preparedness, and home hardening awareness. Technology and innovation: integration of drone technology, real-time mapping, automated hot-spot detection systems; implementation of the Genasys Protect system, enhancing our ability to issue geographically targeted evacuation alerts and updates. Alternative water source training: every field member is now trained on how to utilize pools, reservoirs, and auxiliary tanks as backup water sources when hydrants are compromised."

He closed with a forward-looking assessment:

"These changes represent more than operational tweaks. They reflect a cultural shift toward a proactive, data driven, and technology enhanced firefighting approach. The Palisades Fire reinforced that the Los Angeles Fire Department is facing a new reality. Fire season no longer exists in the traditional sense—it is now a year-round threat. Extreme wind events, high fuel loads, prolonged drought have combined to make our wildland-urban interface increasingly vulnerable. What does this mean? It means we must continue to invest in training, infrastructure, personnel, and technology to stay ahead of the next incident. We're working with regional partners to standardize terminology, response thresholds, evacuation triggers, ensuring consistency across jurisdictions when future large-scale fires occur. In closing, this review is not simply a reflection of what happened. It is a commitment to what comes next. It honors the extraordinary courage of our firefighters and the resilience of the Palisades community. I want to send a message to the residents of the Palisades: we stand with you. I want to send a message to our firefighters: your professionalism under extreme conditions represents the very best of this department. The Palisades Fire will be remembered not only for its destruction, but also for the dedication, innovation, and teamwork that defined our response. We're stronger today because of what we faced. We're more prepared because of what we learned, and we are united as one team moving toward a safer, more resilient Los Angeles. That concludes my summary of the AAR."

Later, Everett shared something his father had said after watching the fire unfold: "That was the biggest fire there ever was—and ever will be."

Everett did not dispute the sentiment. His leadership, combined with the transparency of the After-Action Review, underscored the broader reality: the Palisades Fire was not just a wind-driven wildfire. It tested systems, readiness, and capabilities. The broader examination of those forces continued later that month at a symposium dedicated to wind-driven wildfires and the infrastructure they confront.

Erik Scott

Chapter 20

CHIEFS' PLAYBOOK FOR A WIND-DRIVEN CITY

"Wind-Driven Wildland Urban Interface Fires and Infrastructure Resilience"

~ Cal State LA Symposium, October 30, 2025

The auditorium at California State University, Los Angeles, was filled with engineers, policy students, and public-safety professionals—a cross-section of the people who build, manage, and protect the city. The event brought together experts to examine the science and coordination behind modern firestorms.

Among the keynote speakers were two of Southern California's foremost wildfire subject-matter experts: Assistant Chief Guy Tomlinson, Los Angeles Fire Department, Special Operations, and Division Chief Oscar Vargas, U.S. Forest Service, Angeles National Forest. Both have decades of line and command experience in some of the most complex wildland-urban interface (WUI) incidents in the nation.

Tomlinson opened with humor that masked a hard truth.

"It's a beautiful day. You can see the mountains," he said. "Now open your pocketbook—we have to staff extra today, and we haven't even had an incident."

Erik Scott

The point landed. Readiness costs money before the smoke. Helicopters, dozers, and strike teams don't appear on command; they're pre-positioned, funded, and fueled long before the first spark.

"Everything we do," Tomlinson added, "comes back to relationships. You can't meet your partners for the first time on scene."

Vargas followed with the broader view from the Angeles National Forest. "This landscape wants to burn. Fire is part of it. We built the urban part inside it."

He reminded the audience that Los Angeles isn't a city bordered by wilderness—it is wilderness stitched with city grids. The brush, grass, and palm canopy have always adapted to fire; humans haven't. The result is the WUI problem: natural terrain meeting combustible infrastructure, where a single wind-driven ember can ignite a neighborhood.

Tomlinson and Vargas dissected what made the January 2025 events—Palisades, Eaton, and others—so destructive. Both referenced the Particularly Dangerous Situation (PDS) Red-Flag forecast that preceded those fires, a meteorological classification rarely used in Southern California.

The winds, they explained, didn't just push flames forward—they widened them. Path of least resistance became the map. Canyons vented airflow like turbines; palm fronds turned into ember launchers; pine needles in gutters became linear fuses down entire streets. In that environment, even a well-planned defense line could be jumped in seconds.

They emphasized that these were no longer "wildfires" in the traditional sense but urban firestorms—hundreds of homes burning simultaneously across miles of roadway. Engines were blocked by downed lines and trees; firefighters made rescues in near-zero visibility. The goal shifted to survival and triage.

Their presentation underscored that Southern California's success lies in a relentless, system-wide discipline:

- Shared Weather Picture. Agencies meet with the National Weather Service before and during every season to unify forecast language, trigger points, and public alerts.
- Common Radio Nets. Every morning, dispatch centers from Los Angeles City, County, Ventura, Verdugo, and the Angeles National Forest conduct a live check on V-FIRE 21, the regional mutual-aid channel. The 10:00 a.m. ritual ensures instant interoperability when the next column rises.
- Unified Command Structure. The chiefs described incidents where up to seven agencies operated as one. Co-location at a single Incident Command Post—with shared objectives, resource ordering, and evacuation language—prevents overlap of parallel commands.
- Technology with Accountability. Tools such as Genasys Protect, Tablet Command, and shared CAD bridges now link local, state, and federal systems so that an update in one platform populates across many others.
- Continuous Drills. The Foothill Mutual Threat Zone (MTZ) and Santa Susana MTZ coalitions hold monthly coordination meetings and annual large-scale evacuation exercises. What looks like instant response is built from those repetitions.

Tomlinson spoke bluntly about cost and consequence of pre-positioning additional resources on high-hazard days. "That quarter-million dollars we spend on readiness today," he said, "is a down payment on lives we won't lose tomorrow."

Both chiefs also addressed the long tail of recovery—the tension between the urgency to repopulate and the lingering hazards of ash, unstable slopes, and contaminated water systems. "You have to rebuild, but you have to bring people back safely," Vargas said. "That balance is the hardest part."

Later that day, I took the stage as one of the symposium's lecturers to discuss emergency public information—how messaging itself can function as a life-safety tool when it is timely, accurate, and consistent. The conversation that began with physics and command strategy ended with communication: science and words working together to keep people safe.

The Cal State LA event reaffirmed what many of us already knew from the fireground:

- Wind, fuel, and topography dictate behavior, but relationships determine success.
- Unified Command and Unified Messaging are not bureaucratic layers—they are lifelines.
- Preparedness is cumulative. Every pre-season drill, weather call, and daily radio test pays off when a city is tested.
- Recovery requires honesty. Getting residents home quickly means little if they return to unseen hazards.

None of it was theoretical. It was the same quiet professionalism that defines Los Angeles' multi-agency wildfire response—the behind-the-scenes architecture of readiness that the public rarely sees but depends on every time the wind turns offshore.

The symposium reinforced how wind, infrastructure, and coordination determine outcomes long before the first spark. But even with the best science and tactics, one challenge remained constant: how we communicate during these events. Before the Palisades Fire, that challenge had led me to develop a system that now serves as the city's foundation for clear, unified messaging—Unified LA.

Chapter 21

UNIFIED LA: ONE CLEAR VOICE

**"If Los Angeles didn't speak with one voice,
people could pay the price."**

~ Erik Scott

The responsibility of sending clear messaging during a disaster didn't begin with the Palisades Fire. Years earlier, when I was still serving at firefighter rank, I had been unexpectedly thrust into one of the department's most elite arenas. Battalion Chief Carlos Calvillo had just been promoted to Assistant Chief, and with his new role, he stepped away from the Fire Incident Management Team (FIMT). Unbeknownst to me, he sent a formal email to the Emergency Operations Commander recommending that I take his place.

When I found out, I was honored, humbled—and honestly, scared. The FIMT was filled with subject matter experts and seasoned leaders—the "heavy hitters" of the LAFD. I didn't feel worthy to sit at that table. I told Chief Calvillo as much, and he said something I never forgot. Simple yet profound:

"Erik, it's all about the relationships."

At the time, I nodded, but the meaning didn't sink in. Only later did I realize how right he was. Trust and respect—those relationships—are the backbone of disaster response. Without them, information bottlenecks and coordination can falter.

Another challenge was gnawing at me. On long-duration, multi-agency incidents under a unified command, it was often unclear which department should put out the message. Fire? Police? Emergency Management? Transportation? Everyone had their own channels, and that fractured messaging often confused the very people we were trying to protect.

The public needed clarity. They needed one clear, vetted voice.

This aha moment was the seed of what became Unified LA—a system I conceived to force consistency across agencies so credibility wouldn't erode when the city needed it most. After developing the concept, I presented it to the Incident Management Team, received approval, and built out both the framework and the social media platforms that carried its message. At the time, it was purely instinct—an understanding that if Los Angeles didn't speak with one voice, people could pay the price.

What started as an experiment grew into a cornerstone. Over the past decade, *Unified LA* has been activated during some of Los Angeles's biggest emergencies:

- Massive wildfires, where hundreds of thousands relied on real-time evacuation orders.
- Large-scale protests, where multiple agencies operated under unified command and public trust depended on consistency.
- Tropical storms, where accurate and steady messaging guided people through flooding and outages.

The Los Angeles Marathon—where Unified LA served as the official source for status updates, safety information, and transit impacts across multiple cities and jurisdictions.

I was honored to play a role in the creation of Unified LA, but countless others—from the city's communication professionals to agency partners—helped refine and elevate it into what it is today.

Unified LA isn't "my idea" anymore. It's an institutional tool of the City of Los Angeles—a model for cutting through the noise in an age when misinformation travels faster than fire. Looking back, I see the arc clearly: a firefighter who once questioned his own worth, a mentor who taught me that everything comes down to relationships, and a system that now helps millions when disaster strikes.

Unified LA strengthened how agencies communicate. But communication is only part of preparedness. Just as the city must speak with one voice, the public must understand how to act when that voice calls. Those lessons—and how to teach them—form the backbone of our approach to disaster readiness.

Chapter 22

LESSONS IN DISASTER PREPAREDNESS

"Disaster preparedness isn't just a checklist—it's a mindset."

~ Erik Scott

Disasters don't wait for perfect conditions and preparation can determine outcomes. In the fire service, there's a few training truths we've learned along the way:

- You may not rise to the level of the incident; you may fall to the level of your training.
- Train as if your life depends on it, because it does.
- The most important thing we do is respond to emergencies, the second most important thing we do is train for them.

For the public, "training" takes a different form, but the stakes are the same. Preparation is what the public falls back on when disaster hits: hardened homes, evacuation routes, go-kits, practiced plans, and trusted information.

This chapter focuses on readiness in all its forms, because across disasters, the principles—early action, planning, and resilient infrastructure—are universal.

Here's an important micro-lesson on being prepared for fire season—*Ready, Set, Go.*

- **Ready**: Harden your home and prep your go-kit before red-flag days. Photograph rooms for insurance. Know two exit routes.

- **Set**: Park facing out. Load the Six P's (see below). Keep shoes by the door.
- **Go:** Leave early. Early beats perfect. Traffic doubles the danger. If you wonder "Is it time?"—it's time.

Wildfire conditions can shift from calm to catastrophic in minutes.

- Once heavy smoke reduces visibility, even familiar streets become disorienting.
- Never wait for flames to appear before leaving.
- If authorities issue an Evacuation Warning, be prepared to leave. If an Evacuation Order is issued, depart immediately.
- Keep routes clear, maintain situational awareness, and remember: the safest rescue is the one that never has to be made.

Evacuations That Worked

Tens of thousands of residents evacuated safely. Assisted-living facilities were moved by bus, escorted by fire and police units. On Sunset Blvd. and Pacific Coast Highway, LAPD directed traffic to the south, away from the fire front, while dozers cleared abandoned cars to open escape lanes for strike teams.

Evacuations often get overlooked in the story of a fire, but in this case, they worked as designed. People listened, followed the guidance, and lives were saved.

This kind of success doesn't happen by accident. It's the result of drills, signage, inter-agency coordination, and public trust. These same principles apply to hurricanes (where contraflow lanes reverse traffic), floods (where early warnings trigger shelter-in-place or vertical evacuation), and earthquakes (where Drop, Cover, Hold On, clear exit routes, and reunification plans matter). The takeaway: evacuation isn't just about leaving—it's about knowing when, where, and how to go.

Micro-Lesson — The Six P's of Evacuation

When it's time to leave, don't hesitate. Grab the Six P's:

- **People & Pets** – family members, animals, leashes, carriers.
- **Papers** – IDs, passports, insurance documents.
- **Prescriptions** – medications, eyeglasses, medical devices.
- **Photos** – irreplaceable albums, heirlooms.
- **Personal Devices** – phones, laptops, chargers.
- **Plastic** – credit cards, cash.

Why it matters: Panic fogs judgment. Having the Six P's ready turns a scramble into a plan, and a plan can be lifesaving.

Home Hardening Basics

Back in Chapter One, I explained that most homes aren't lost to walls of flame but to embers carried by the wind. I first recognized the life-saving power of home hardening during the 2018 Woolsey Fire.

I was deployed for nearly two weeks and drove through the North Ranch area of Westlake Village. The image stays with me: one home burned to the ground, the house across the street untouched. This wasn't the flame front. It was embers, pushed by powerful Santa Ana winds, finding vulnerabilities where homes weren't hardened.

Embers vs. Flame Front

Wind-driven embers can travel blocks or even miles ahead of the flame front. They slip through small vulnerabilities—gutters, vents, doormats, or fences tied directly into the house. One ember in the wrong spot can reduce a home to ash, even when the flame front never touches it.

Why it matters: At your house, the battle is predominately against embers.

Home hardening—the small, often overlooked details—can make the difference between homes that stand and homes that don't.

Here are some basics:

- **Roof:** Class A fire-rated material (composition, metal, tile). Keep it clear of debris.
- **Vents:** Cover with ⅛" or finer metal mesh to block ember entry.
- **Gutters:** Clean out leaves and pine needles; use non-combustible guards.
- **Windows:** Dual-pane, tempered glass resists heat longer.
- **Decks & Fencing:** Keep clear of debris underneath; break wooden fencing before it ties into the house.
- **Defensible Space:** Maintain lean, clean landscaping in the 5–30 foot zone; reduce fuels out to 200 feet in Los Angeles.

Why it matters: We'd love to park a fire engine in front of every home during a wildfire, but that's not possible. Brush clearance is how you join our team. We provide the offense; you provide the defense. Create a defensible space around your home. Focus on clearing the ground fuels. Shape your vegetation so everything looks like a lollipop—canopy up high, everything else down to 3 inches. That space is what gives us firefighters a chance to save your home when embers arrive.

California's Zone 0 Regulation

In response to rising wildfire threats, California is finalizing its most aggressive home safety regulation yet: Zone 0, the first five feet around a structure. This ember-resistant zone is designed to eliminate the most common ignition pathways—mulch, wooden fences, flammable plants, and debris—that allow embers to leap from ground to home.

Here's what Zone 0 means in practice:

- **No combustible materials** within five feet of the home—this includes mulch, stacked firewood, and most vegetation.
- **Exceptions** may include potted plants and well-maintained mature trees, provided branches are pruned at least five feet above the roofline.
- **Applies to new construction immediately** in high-risk zones; existing homes will have three years to comply.
- **Insurance incentives** are being explored to reward compliance and improve coverage access.

This regulation is controversial. In dense urban areas, five feet may be the entire distance between homes. In communities where shade is scarce, removing hedges and shrubs raises concerns about heat and aesthetics. But the science is clear: embers are the leading cause of home ignition during wildfires, and Zone 0 is a direct response to that threat.

Why it matters: Zone 0 isn't just about fire—it's about resilience. It's about giving homeowners a clear, actionable way to protect their property. And it's about shifting the narrative from reaction to prevention.

Brush Clearance Done Right

I saw the stakes firsthand during the 2017 Mandeville Canyon fire, which ignited when a well-intentioned resident sparked a blaze while clearing brush. Brush clearance protects homes when done wisely, but on the wrong day—or with the wrong tools—it can be just as dangerous as doing nothing at all.

- **When to work:** Cool, moist mornings are safest. Avoid hot, dry, or windy afternoons.

- **How to work:** In Los Angeles' Very High Fire Hazard Severity Zones, metal cutting blades for brush clearance are restricted to non-sparking types. On red-flag days, metal blades and gas-powered equipment with hot exhaust are frequent ignition sources. Always have water or a fire extinguisher close at hand.
- **How far to clear:** Most of California requires 100 feet of defensible space; Los Angeles requires 200 feet.
- **Why it matters:** One spark in the wrong conditions can erase an entire neighborhood.

Mudslide Safety

- **Know the Warning Signs:** Rills forming on hillsides, water turning brown with debris, or small rockfalls can signal larger slides coming.
- **Obey Evacuation Orders:** They're issued for a reason. If you're told to leave, go before the roads close.
- **Never Drive Through Flooded Roads:** Water mixed with mud and debris hides depth and strength. *Turn Around, Don't Drown.*
- **Burn Scars Multiply Risk:** Vegetation is gone, the soil is water-repellent, and slopes fail faster. Be especially cautious in the first rainy seasons after a fire.

Disaster preparedness isn't just a checklist—it's a mindset. It's how we show up for our families, our neighbors, and ourselves when the stakes are highest. Whether it's packing the Six P's, clearing brush with intention, or rethinking the first five feet around our homes, every action we take before a crisis is an act of care. The lessons from fire zones apply across emergencies: plan early, act decisively, and build readiness into the everyday. Because when the next disaster comes—and it will—preparedness won't just protect property. It will protect lives.

Erik Scott

Chapter 23

LEADERSHIP UNDER FIRE

*"Leadership is about showing up, setting the tone,
and strengthening people to be greater than
they believed they could be."*

~ *Erik Scott*

L eadership in the fire service is not theoretical. It's lived in smoke, sweat, and difficult choices. Over our careers, many of us have learned that leadership is less about rank on your collar and more about how you earn trust, steady a team, and make decisions under pressure. Those lessons didn't come from a classroom alone. They came from real life experiences, failures, moments of clarity in chaos, and from leading alongside some of the most dedicated people we know.

We anchor our leadership philosophy in a simple truth: our members are our most valuable resource. Period. Equipment, strategy, and technology matter, but it's people who carry the mission. That belief shapes how we lead. We never ask something of others that we are not willing to do ourselves. We study our craft, because credibility comes from competence. And above all, we take care of our people—protect them, advocate for them, and set them up to succeed.

One of the most effective ways to grow as a leader is to see the workplace through the eyes of the team. Only then can we identify what can be improved, and more importantly, empower people to be part of the solution. Two assumptions guide that approach. First, there is often a better way to do things. Second—contrary to tradition—the crew's insights might be more profound than the captain's. The people closest to the work often see inefficiencies, opportunities, or blind spots that leadership might unintentionally overlook.

We've also learned that it's better to involve the team earlier rather than later. If a leader builds out a detailed plan before asking for input, it becomes harder—practically and psychologically—to pivot when ideas diverge. The more time invested in a plan, the harder it is to adjust. But when people are brought in at the outset, we not only capture their best thinking, we gain their buy-in from the very beginning. The real secret to lasting change lies in building systems and processes that people actually want to carry out. When they feel ownership—because they've shaped the path forward—the results are not only better but also sustainable.

Over the years, we've seen leaders succeed and others stumble. The difference is often whether they have a clear philosophy that matches their actions. Praise, for instance, is infinitely more powerful than punishment. Recognition delayed until retirement parties, funerals, or after a serious injury is too late. People need to hear they are valued while they are still in the fight. That doesn't mean ignoring the few who refuse to meet expectations. In those rare cases, clear documentation and accountability are necessary. But most of the time, positive reinforcement builds strength far faster than punishment ever will.

Leadership has been described as a bank account: every time you mentor, advocate, or show up for your team, you make a deposit into credibility. Every mistake or misstep is a withdrawal. We're all human—we all make withdrawals—but the hope is that we've built enough capital that one mistake doesn't bankrupt us. Leadership, at its core, is relational, not positional.

We've also seen how leadership shifts depending on context. On a fireground, you may have to be autocratic—there's no time for debate when flames are moving faster than cars can drive. At a community meeting, you lean diplomatic, because people need to be heard and reassured. And sometimes, when it's just choosing where the crew will grab lunch, you can lean away from bureaucracy and let the group decide. Good leaders are situational leaders. They know when to direct, when to listen, and when to step back.

Much of our approach to leadership was shaped by people who left their mark on the department. One enduring framework came from John Drake, a former second-in-command who taught a Captain's class early in our careers. His material stayed with us. He introduced a simple acronym that became a touchstone for building strong crews: MOTIVATE.

- **Mentor:** Guide people not just for the task in front of them, but for the career ahead. Mentorship is an investment in their growth and in the future of the organization.
- **Open Door Policy:** Maintain one that functions in practice, not just in theory. Success only works when crews feel welcome to bring forward questions, frustrations, and even mistakes without fear of reprisal.
- **Trust:** Trust is currency. When members know they are trusted, they take ownership, think ahead, and contribute at a higher level.
- **Included:** Involve your team in decisions whenever possible. Inclusion builds clarity, reduces friction, and strengthens commitment because people support what they help

create.

- **Valued:** Make sure people know their contributions matter. When members feel valued, their sense of ownership grows, and their performance elevates.
- **Accountable:** Set clear expectations and follow through. Accountability is not punishment—it is the structure that makes empowerment safe and standards meaningful.
- **Teach:** Share the "why," not just the "what." Teaching the principles behind decisions equips your team to act with confidence and consistency when you're not standing next to them.
- **Empower** Give people the tools, authority, and confidence to act. When empowered, they will rise higher than they thought possible and often exceed even your expectations.

When members feel mentored, trusted, valued, and empowered, their potential expands. Accountability is the backbone. Recognition is the fuel. Recognition motivates more powerfully than discipline ever will.

Another touchstone came from Captain D. Michael Abrashoff's book *It's Your Ship*. His philosophy is that leaders thrive not by barking orders but by creating climates of trust, listening aggressively, looking for results instead of salutes, and improving people's quality of life. That approach fit naturally into the fire service. Our goal is always to win trust and eventually the enthusiastic commitment of the team to a shared mission. Promotions and recognition go to innovators and pioneers, not to those who cling to comfort and avoid improvement. Stasis is death to any organization. We evolve, or we die.

We studied these concepts in depth at the Los Angeles Fire Department Leadership Academy, a 136-hour graduate-level program adapted from West Point. Among the most valuable tools we practiced was Leader's Intent. Rooted in military doctrine, it breaks down into three parts: the Task—what needs to be done; the Purpose—why it needs to be done; and the End State—what success looks like. Leader's Intent provides clarity in chaos. When radios fail or conditions shift, firefighters can adapt because they know the outcome we're aiming for. It's not micromanagement. It's empowerment within boundaries.

Leadership is also about structure, not just philosophy. In the fire service, we use a model called the Standards of Command, remembered through the phrase ASCRIBE To the Standards of Command. It's how we bring order to chaos, and it applies far beyond the fireground. Whether you're making decisions at home, managing a team, or leading during a crisis, the same principles help you slow down, get organized, and move with purpose.

- **A - Assume Command** Take responsibility for the problem in front of you. Don't wait for someone else to step in.
- **S - Situational Awareness** Get the facts. Understand what's happening before you make a move.
- **C - Communications** Make sure everyone involved knows the plan. Clear communication prevents confusion.
- **R - Resource Deployment** Use what you have—people, tools, time—wisely and efficiently.
- **I - Incident Objectives & Action Plan** Define the goal and outline the steps. What does success look like?
- **B - Be Organized (with Incident Command System)** Break the problem into parts. Assign roles. Don't try to handle everything alone.
- **E - Evaluate & Revise** Check your progress. Adjust as needed. Flexibility prevents small issues from becoming big ones.

Erik Scott

- **T - Transfer Command** When someone more qualified arrives—or when circumstances change—hand off the responsibility smoothly. Continuity matters.

These steps help firefighters manage complex emergencies, but they also help families handle stressful moments and leaders navigate difficult decisions. ASCRIBE To, gives everyone a framework to stay calm, think clearly, and act with purpose when it matters most.

The Palisades Fire tested every one of these frameworks. What carried us forward wasn't perfection—it was discipline. Leader's intent kept objectives clear when radios failed. ASCRIBE To the Standards of Command provided a structure when conditions shifted faster than any plan could keep pace. And the principle of putting key people in key places proved decisive, as logistics anticipated shortages before they broke us, strike teams anchored lines at natural breaks, and public information officers synchronized evacuation messaging with law enforcement.

The outcomes weren't measured in flawless execution—they rarely are in chaos. They were measured in lives saved, neighborhoods protected, and crews that stayed united under impossible conditions. That is what leadership looks like when it's tested: intent, trust, and disciplined execution bending the outcome, even when the storm itself can't be stopped.

The truth is this: leadership doesn't stop at the edge of the fireground. The same lessons apply in boardrooms, classrooms, and living rooms. The details of the mission may change—profit margins instead of fire perimeters, student growth instead of evacuation numbers—but the fundamentals don't. Lead by example and you create credibility. Give purpose and you create buy-in. Build trust and you create resilience. Empower people and you create momentum.

Leadership isn't about collar brass, corner offices, or titles on business cards. It's about showing up, setting the tone, and building people to be stronger than they thought they could be. Whether under hurricane-force winds in Los Angeles or in the daily grind of managing teams elsewhere, leadership under fire is leadership, period.

Erik Scott

Chapter 24

REFLECTION AND RESOLVE

"Even under hurricane winds and firestorm skies, Los Angeles
stood together. Undaunted. Unbroken. Resilient."

~ *Erik Scott*

When I look back on the Palisades Fire, what strikes me most is
not just the destruction—but the resilience. I can still see the hills
glowing, the neighborhoods reduced to a forest of chimneys, and
the families returning to ash. It was devastating. And yet, I can also
see what we saved: tens of thousands of people evacuated safely,
thousands of homes still standing, and a city that refused to break
under impossible conditions.

The Palisades Fire broke out under extraordinary circumstances: hurricane-level winds gusting close to 100 miles per hour,
humidity near zero, and vegetation pushed to tinder-dry conditions after years of drought. Add to that the steep terrain of the Santa Monica Mountains and simultaneous fires across the region—the
Sunset, Eaton, and Hurst—and the stage was set for one of the most
complex firefights in the city's history.

No department had faced this exact combination of extremes.
And yet from the very first call, firefighters ran toward the danger.
Within 30 minutes, hundreds of additional resources had been re-
quested. Helicopters were over the fire in 10 minutes. Mutual-aid

partners mobilized almost instantly.

There were moments that tested us. In the first 24 hours, resources were strained under the weight of simultaneous incidents. Traffic clogged evacuation routes, forcing bulldozers to clear the way for engines.

But every challenge was met with adaptation. When terrain and weather conspired against us, tactical patrols leapfrogged into neighborhoods, stamping out embers before they could take entire blocks.

In those critical first 36 hours, 30,000 residents were evacuated safely. For every home lost, two or more were saved. Pilots flew into winds that shredded water drops mid-air, and ground crews held the line in cul-de-sacs and canyons under extraordinary pressure.

Those victories are easy to overlook in the shadow of destruction. But they matter. They are the difference between a city scarred and a city broken—and Los Angeles was not broken. Injuries to firefighters remained minimal, not because the fire was forgiving, but because training, discipline, and safety protocols never wavered, even in chaos.

~~~~~

The Palisades Fire revealed gaps—just as all major incidents do. Those lessons are already shaping reforms and strengthening how we prepare for the next challenge. We are committed to refining the system because lives depend on it.

But equally important is the lesson of courage. I saw firefighters refuse to yield when the fire bent physics itself—when hose streams curved sideways, and embers rained like missiles. I saw neighbors helping neighbors evacuate. I saw a city lean on its first responders, and first responders lean on each other.

When the fire was finally contained, we felt the weight of all that was lost. But we also felt pride in what we had saved. This fire will be remembered as one of Los Angeles' darkest chapters—marked not only by tragedy, but by the resilience of those who fought to protect the city and those who endured it.

Calm proved contagious. It wasn't passive—it was deliberate, disciplined, steady. Crews mirrored it. Residents leaned on it. Calm turned panic into order, and order into survival.

The Palisades Fire tested us. It scarred our hillsides and our hearts. But it also proved something powerful: that even under hurricane winds and firestorm skies, Los Angeles stands together. Undaunted. Unbroken. Resilient. Showing what is possible when a city stands united and moves forward as one.

Erik Scott

A neighborhood is consumed on both sides of the street as wind-driven flames roar through large homes, turning this once-quiet residential corner into a tunnel of fire. Credit: MySafeLA Greg Doyle

An LAFD firefighter cooling hot spots and extinguishing remaining embers after a structure was heavily damaged during the Palisades Fire. Credit: LAFD Photographer ll G. Apodaca

Erik Scott

An LAFD firefighter pushes through the front gate of a burning residence, advancing a hose line toward the heart of the fire despite extreme heat and collapse hazards. Credit: MySafeLA Greg Doyle

An LAFD helicopter attempts a water drop, but the strong winds push the stream sideways and evaporate much of it before it reaches the target area below. Credit: MySafeLA Greg Doyle

Firefighters confront a fully involved residence under extreme wind-driven conditions while simultaneously protecting the adjacent home to the left during the Palisades Fire. Credit: LAFD

Erik Scott

Incident Command officers coordinate operations during the Palisades Fire, mapping fire movement and tactical priorities in real time as conditions rapidly evolved. Credit: LAFD Photographer ll G. Apodaca

Los Angeles Fire Captain Erik Scott MC'ing a Unified Command press conference as multiple agencies coordinated response efforts during the Palisades Fire.

Firefighters work aggressively from a hillside property to knock down advancing flames as thick smoke fills the sky, while nearby residents assist with garden hoses in a coordinated effort to protect homes during a fast-moving brush fire. CreditLAFD

LAFD firefighters battle a fully involved garage as wind-driven flames consume the structure, working to stop the fire's spread deeper into the neighborhood. Credit: MySafeLA Greg Doyle

Erik Scott

Wind-driven fire overruns a hillside neighborhood, igniting multiple homes as the sun cuts through thick smoke and embers.
Credit: MySafeLA Greg Doyle

LAFD Engine 221 uses a Wagon Battery Tourette defensively along Pacific Coast Highway as intense winds push flames toward nearby structures during the Palisades Fire. Photo credit: LAFD

Calm Amidst Chaos

Epilogue

If there's one thing I hope you carry from these pages, it's that resilience is possible—even when we're wounded, even in the fiercest storm.

The Palisades Fire tested our city, the department, and me personally in ways I never could have imagined. It pushed us to our limits, challenged our assumptions, and demanded a level of endurance few had ever experienced. But it also revealed something remarkable: what calm, courage, and genuine care for one another can achieve when everything is on the line.

I witnessed firefighters who were exhausted, smoke-covered, and emotionally spent still finding a way to lift each other up. I saw neighbors supporting neighbors, communities stepping forward, and people choosing compassion in moments when it would have been easier to break apart. Those acts of quiet strength—rarely captured by cameras or reports—are what carried us through.

This book isn't just about fire. It's about finding clarity when the world feels overwhelming. It's about standing steady when others lean on you, and knowing when to lean on others yourself. It's about the relationships built long before a crisis—friendships, partnerships, and simple human connections—that become lifelines when everything begins to shake.

And it's about remembering that leadership—whether on a

Erik Scott

fireline, in a boardroom, or in your own family—begins with *Calm Amidst Chaos*. Real leadership doesn't demand the spotlight; it shows up in the steady voice, the quiet decision, the patient pause, and the willingness to care for people even when you're hurting too.

My hope is that these lessons stay with you. That they remind you of the strength we share, even when shaken. And that when your own storms come, you'll meet them with steadiness, compassion, and courage—grounded in the knowledge that we are always strongest when we stand together.

Stay safe. Stay sharp.
~ *Erik Scott*

Acknowledgements

My deepest thanks go to my wife, Lauren, for her unwavering support and for being my rock throughout this journey.

To Ruthie Smith, for showing me that writing a book was possible. And to my parents and family, who became spontaneous, unpaid proofreaders—compensated entirely in hugs.

To Cheryl Benton and her small but mighty publishing team, your guidance was invaluable.

To my mentors, who have taught me so much and whose wisdom I strive to pay forward every day, thank you for guiding me on this path.

To my fellow public information officers, who work tirelessly to keep the public informed and safe—your dedication inspires me.

To Eric Garcetti, Robert Kovacik, Frank Lima, and Larry Vein—thank you for your generous endorsements and for believing in this story.

A heartfelt thank you to Sean Penn for his grit and tenacity in helping others, and for lending his support and encouragement to this project.

And finally, to the LAFD colleagues and residents who entrusted me with their stories—this book is as much yours as it is mine. Thank you for your bravery and your truth.

Erik Scott

About the Author

Erik Scott is a Captain II / Paramedic and the senior, longest-serving lead Public Information Officer for the Los Angeles Fire Department. With more than two decades of fire service experience, he has become a trusted voice in times of crisis—most notably during the Palisades Fire, when his calm, clear updates guided millions through one of Southern California's most challenging wildfire emergencies.

A qualified Type 1 PIO—the highest level of certification—Scott has responded to nearly every type of emergency imaginable, working alongside the dedicated men and women of the LAFD. He began his career as the Top Overall Recruit and went on to earn an Associate of Science degree in Emergency Medical Services and a Bachelor of Science degree in Emergency Services Management, graduating with a perfect 4.0 GPA. His professional development includes serving as a UCLA paramedic instructor, training as a Terrorism Liaison Officer, and completing the West Point LAFD Leadership Academy.

Scott has conducted tens of thousands of media interviews with local, national, and international outlets, and is frequently deployed to support major wildfires and large-scale disasters as part of Incident Management Teams. A sought-after speaker on crisis communication, he continues to highlight the teamwork and dedication of firefighters and partner agencies, embodying leadership, clarity under pressure, and genuine concern for the communities he serves.

www.ingramcontent.com/pod-product-compliance
Lightning Source LLC
Chambersburg PA
CBHW070910130626
46555CB00001B/75